Comparative Labor Movements

Ideological Roots and Institutional Development

Adolf Sturmthal
University of Illinois

D1568958

Wadsworth Publishing Company, Inc.
Belmont, California

Design: Gary A. Head

Editing: Sandra Craig/Kevin Gleason

Cover: Steve Renick

© 1972 by Wadsworth Publishing Company, Inc., Belmont, California 94002. All rights reserved. No part of this book may
be reproduced, stored in a retrieval system or transcribed, in
any form or by any means, electronic, mechanical, photocopying,
recording or otherwise, without the prior written permission of
the publisher.

ISBN-0-534-00193-9

L. C. Cat. Card No.: 72-84789

Printed in the United States of America

1 2 3 4 5 6 7 8 9 10—76 75 74 73 72

To keep the price of this book as low as possible, we have used
an economical means of typesetting. We welcome your comments.

331. 8809
5936 c

164237

Series Foreword

Many of today's serious social issues are arising in and are profoundly modifying the labor market and its institutions. These issues include the rights and welfare of ethnic minorities; unionization of white-collar and professional people and strikes in vital public services; inflation, economic growth, and unemployment; automation and job training; antitrust, conglomerates, and coalition bargaining; the injection of heavier doses of union democracy into the collective bargaining process —to name a few. Hence, the labor market provides an excellent "laboratory" for the study of social change.

The analytic techniques now being applied to these problems, however, require new teaching materials. Due weight must be given to these exciting new approaches, for the contemporary undergraduate or graduate student is far less inclined than was his predecessor to sip such new wine out of an old bottle—in this case, the overstuffed and often stultifying text book. Instructors too (including the undersigned), chafe at the inevitable restraint imposed by the textbook's unitary approach, selection of topics, and order of presentation. Recourse to the library for "supplementary" materials is becoming increasingly difficult and frustrating.

We have tried in this series to alleviate, and we hope eliminate, some of these problems. These books make it easier for the instructor to select specific areas for study and, where necessary, to eliminate others in a particular course. They offer him latitude in arranging the *sequence* of topics according to his own preferences and requirements, as well as a variety of approaches and an opportunity for critical discussion. The viewpoints and approaches of the authors in this series are by no means uniform and homogeneous; nor has any attempt been made to make them so. Neither have we sought to avoid occasional overlapping, which would in any event be unavoidable. What we have attempted to avoid is monotony and the

staleness which can occur when traditional staple fare is up-
dated merely by tacking on additional chapters to deal with
new problems as they emerge.

LLOYD ULLMAN
 Professor of Economics
 Director, Institute of Industrial
 Relations
 University of California,
 Berkeley

GEORGE STRAUSS
 Professor of Business
 Administration
 Associate Director, Institute of
 Industrial Relations
 University of California,
 Berkeley

Preface

It would be difficult to find any period in American history when knowledge of foreign and international labor movements and the industrial relations systems of other countries was more urgently needed than the present. True, the Vietnam War has undoubtedly produced a tendency among many Americans to turn away from international commitments and to concentrate their attention upon our many pressing domestic problems. Yet, whether we like it or not, our involvement in international affairs remains a fundamental fact of life. And the labor movements abroad, in the wider sense in which this term is used in the pages that follow, are factors of such significance in the international community that they can be disregarded only at great risk.

Some of the most important and difficult problems which confront this country are common to most, if not all, of the industrially advanced nations, even though different traditions and ideologies may produce differences in the way in which these problems are being viewed and tackled. There is a good deal to be learned from foreign experience, both about policies that worked and about others that failed.

This book is intended to be an introduction to this large body of knowledge. Part One presents the background of the European labor movements in so far as it is necessary for an understanding of contemporary problems. Part Two explores various European collective bargaining systems and some of the main problems which they face. Among them we examine especially the relationship between workers' councils and unions, the role of unions in nationalized enterprises, and the difficult issues which full employment brings in its wake; this includes a discussion of various European experiments with "Incomes Policies." In the last part of the book we leave the confines of Europe and devote brief chapters to the international labor movements, especially the tense relations between American and

foreign labor, unionism in socialist countries, and labor in
newly emerging nations.

A concluding chapter attempts to point out some generalizations that may enable us to chart, at least tentatively, the
future course of foreign labor. The brief bibliography will,
I hope, assist the reader in pursuing further any of the topics
discussed in this book.

Two additional comments may be called for. The crisis in
the international labor movement, especially the friction between the AFL-CIO and several of its sister organizations in
Europe, has been further sharpened by the attempts at a merger
of all unions—including those dominated by communists—in Italy. Understandings of some kind with labor organizations in
socialist countries have spread rather rapidly throughout the
West, stimulated in part by the change in the direction of
Washington's foreign policy.

A search for new ideologies in the Western labor organizations accompanies this process of accommodation. The vague
slogan of "participation" has developed a good deal of fascin-
ation for labor, especially those groups that have openly abandoned most of the Marxian traditions.

Almost all of the material in this book is new; the major
exception is a part of the chapter on the nationalized industries, Chapter 9, which appeared previously in *Unity and Diversity in European Labor*, published by the Free Press in 1953.

As an honorable custom requires, I want to thank a number
of people who have read the manuscript and suggested improvements, including the editors of the series of which this book
is a part, Lloyd Ullman and George Strauss, as well as those
who reviewed the manuscript—Professor Val R. Lorwin, University of Oregon, and John P. Windmiller, Cornell University.
Anice Birge, who has mastered the difficult art of deciphering
my handwriting, deserves special acclaim.

Contents

Part One

1

Introduction

The terms *labor movement* and *trade unionism* are used as equivalents in the United States. Any reservations about equating these terms usually refer to whether there is sufficient unity or cooperation among the unions of this country to speak of a labor movement as a cohesive force even in this restricted sense. In most countries, however, the words *labor movement* represent a far wider concept than in the United States. A multitude of organizations—varying from country to country and from one historical period to another—come under that common heading. These are unions, of course, but also political parties (which can be associated in a variety of ways with trade unions), workers' educational organizations, cooperatives (mainly consumers' cooperatives), mutual insurance organizations, workers' sports organizations, and so on, all the way to workers' stamp collectors groups. This diversity of organizations, the relationships between them, and the evolution of these relationships require some explanation if the American student of foreign labor movements and industrial relations systems is to understand their traditions, especially as traditions affect the present operations of the system.

The emphasis in this chapter is on Western and Central Europe, but similar, although not identical, considerations apply to other parts of the world. Tribalism and colonialism are often a counterpart to the specifically European forms of preindustrial societies. The struggle for independence and freedom from colonial oppression plays a role in the evolution of labor movements in the non-Western world similar in many ways to that which the "heroic age" of combat for democratic equality played in the West.

1

Moreover, even within Europe there was considerable diversity of background and of timing in the evolution of labor
movements. To some extent these differences result from the
fact that industrialization came to the various countries at
different times, progressing generally—although with significant exceptions—from west to east and from the center of the
Continent to the north and later to the Mediterranean south,
large parts of which are still in the early stages of this
process or are hardly touched by it. The strength of precapitalistic social, political, and cultural forces and traditions
also varied from country to country, as did the ability of
these earlier social forces to form coalitions with the rising
industrializing classes—or to oppose them. From the stand-
point of an observer in Asia or Africa, European labor movements may manifest a high degree of uniformity; the closer one
moves to the area, however, the more conspicuous are the differences among the various movements, although some variations
may result from leads and lags rather than from permanent distinctions of the evolutionary process.
    Two factors stand out from the many that shaped the evo-
lution of European labor movements: the survival of powerful
feudal and absolutistic elements during the rise of early capitalism, and the impact of the transfer of labor from rural to
industrial activities. Each factor requires some explanation.

CLASS CONSCIOUSNESS

The development of industry and the growth of capitalistic
enterprises proceeded in most countries in Europe under political and social systems which clearly discriminated against labor, but since the twelfth century, when the Cortes of Castile
were meeting, the interests and ideas of the middle classes
gradually found more ways of expression.

> But in what forum could the peasant, the workingman
> speak? He had no representation anywhere, in any
> general or local assembly. . . . [This class] could
> only express itself by insurrection.[1]

The struggle to open channels of expression for the working
class took more than five centuries from the days of Wat Tyler
and the Jacquerie in France before it succeeded in at least the
major countries of Europe.

---

[1]Edward P. Cheyney, *The Dawn of a New Era; 1250-1453* (New York:
Harper & Brothers, 1936), pp. 140-41.

It may come as a surprise to the generation that grew up after World War II that the right of the working class to equal suffrage is in most countries a recent development, often obtained only by a long and bloody struggle. Compared with the United States, Europe gave the workingman equal political status only grudgingly, late, and in stages separated by long intervals. A large part of British labor history, from the Chartist movement in the early nineteenth century to World War I, had as its focus the attainment of the right to vote for the workingman. This evolution, which began with the electoral reform of 1832, was not completed until 1918. Although this process was gradual and for the most part peaceful, British workers were known for their violent demonstrations at the beginning of the nineteenth century, when the political system offered them no other way of influencing legislation and administration.

In Germany the three-class electoral system prevailing in Prussia—the dominant part of the country after its unification in 1871—guaranteed the political control of the country by the upper classes, into which the business groups were gradually absorbed. Essentially the election system made the weight of each man's vote dependent on the taxes he paid. The result was that a small number of wealthy men elected the same number of deputies to the Prussian diet as were elected by workingmen numbering in the millions. This system, with a variant, also existed in Austria-Hungary. Only after the revolutions of 1918 was universal equal suffrage for men and women introduced in Germany and Austria. In Russia the first and only free elections with universal and equal suffrage took place after the revolution of 1917 overthrew Czarist absolutism. Even Sweden—a country now almost universally regarded as a model of democracy—established completely equal suffrage only after World War I, although voting rights had been greatly extended in the wake of a political mass strike early this century. Class consciousness was thus impressed upon the worker by society, and class solidarity proved the key to the attainment of basic human rights.

The restriction of voting rights was one of the most obvious symptoms of discrimination against the worker, but it was neither the only one nor perhaps the most important one. Discrimination extended into every phase of social life. The educational system not only expressed social distinctions but was designed to perpetuate them. Compulsory universal and secular education is, with few exceptions, a relatively recent development, a product of the late nineteenth century or even the early twentieth century. Education beyond the elementary level was reserved for a small part of the younger generation, and university education was the privilege of a select elite, with social background an important selection criterion for a substantial part of the group and intellectual merit a secondary criterion at best. For most working class youth, a university education was until quite recently an unattainable, or even an unthinkable, dream. At the same time, a university degree was and continues to be a requirement for most medium-level and almost all top-level jobs, even outside the professions. Only since World War II has significant progress been made in opening the avenues to higher education to sizeable numbers of children of working class or peasant background, and even now the "lower classes" are vastly underrepresented among university students in most, if not all, European countries.

There were numerous other devices by which the class structure, with its inherent privileges and obligations inherited from the feudal past, survived into the capitalistic stage of European society. In this context, however, the vast scope of this inheritance and the relative ease with which rising capitalism adjusted to this tradition matter less than the fact that in the worker's view the two became intimately tied to one another. To regard the European capitalistic society as ridden with class privileges and organized to keep the worker in his place required no profound social analysis; it corresponded with the everyday experience of the worker.

The dominant institutions of the European society in which modern industry developed emphasized the virtue of submission to its hierarchical order. Not only was it difficult to attempt to move up the social ladder, it was unbecoming as well. Unless a young man had the daring to move out of the security of the family and from the village into a town and to obtain entrance into the process by which artisans were trained, learning and soldiering were the only accepted ways of social advancement. Learning meant primarily preparation for the priesthood and soldiering became a profession at a rather late stage of feudalism. For the bulk of the population, the rules of good conduct far into the nineteenth century were summarized in the German saying, "Cobbler, stay with your last." Against this spirit of quiet submission to one's predestined role in society the pioneers of the European labor movement attempted to mobilize those who were at the bottom of the social pyramid. Whether the material conditions of the workers in the early factories were worse or better than those of the large mass of the rural population has been the subject of prolonged debates. The decline of the death rate which accompanied the rise of the industrial system would seem to indicate that at least in some respects the factory workers were better off than their brethren on the land. No matter; rebellious movements have most often been started by people whose material situation was improving, while their more unfortunate colleagues did not even have the energy necessary for resistance. Moreover, the ranks of

the "industrial slaves of the factory towns"[2] were joined by
master artisans, who were unable to compete with the new factories.

    Rebellion took various forms. Some rebels dreamed of a
return to the life of the preindustrial era; others accepted
modern technology but wanted to turn factory ownership over to
the workers. Some groups of artisans attempted to defend themselves against the new factory systems through the formation of
organizations for joint action, and they ran into the legal
prohibition of "combinations in restraint of trade," which in
one form or another accompanied the early stages of industrialization everywhere. The Combination Act of Great Britain,
the Loi Le Chapelier in France, and various pieces of legislation in the countries that united in 1871 to form the new German Empire prevented, or at least rendered more difficult, the
organization of unions, as did the Common Law doctrine of con-
spiracy in the United States. As a result, the acquisition of
political power in order to make legal the functioning of unions became a primary concern even of labor groups that were
primarily interested in the defense of their economic position.

SOCIALISM OR SYNDICALISM

    In most European countries Socialists emerged as the win-
ners in the struggle for the leadership of the working class.
Socialism, however, was not a uniform doctrine. It appeared in
different forms as presented by a variety of theoreticians—
Saint-Simon, Charles Fourier, Louis Blanc, Robert Owen, Karl
Marx and his associate Friedrich Engels, and many others.
Moreover, the Socialists met powerful rivals in the competition for the leadership of the labor movement—the Anarcho-
Syndicalists. Ideologically, the conflict centered on the role
of the state in the struggle for the emancipation of the work-
ing class.

    For the Anarcho-Syndicalists the state itself was an ene-
my; it had to be destroyed if the workers were to be set free.
The Marxians regarded the state as the most powerful available
instrument for the liberation of the working classes; what mat-
tered was for the workers to obtain control of this instrument.
To destroy the state or to use it for the advancement of the
cause of the workers thus became the main issue between the
Syndicalists and the Marxians.

---

[2]Carl Landauer, *European Socialism: A History of Ideas and
Movements*, Vol. I (Berkeley and Los Angeles: University of California Press), p. 17.

The background for this struggle was the role the state had played in the destruction of the feudal regimes in Europe. Feudal societies were loose federations in which each lord was a small sovereign in his own right, with the king simply one of the lords, the first among equals. By processes that varied from one area to another, the king acquired increased power over the lords, depriving them of all or most of their privileges and functions. A royal army and a civil service took over most of the lords' former functions. Their territory was merged into that of a nation; their serfs became the kings' subjects.

Two processes were essential elements of this transformation: the economic policies labeled *mercantilism* and the growth of a centralized administrative machinery. Mercantilism has been described as a combination of economic policies designed to bring about

> political unification and national power. The building up of nation-states is put in the forefront, and monetary, protectionist, and other economic devices are regarded merely as instruments to this end. State intervention was an essential part of mercantilist doctrine. Those responsible for government accepted mercantilist notions and fashioned their policy accordingly, because they saw in them means of strengthening absolutist states against both the remnants of medieval particularism at home and the rivals abroad.[3]

In our context the salient part of the mercantilist thought is the dominant role it assigned to the state in economic life. Subsidies and the granting of monopoly powers to merchants and industrialists, government intervention in the determination of wages and working conditions, the strict supervision of foreign trade to ensure an export surplus all placed the government in the center of economic life.

The growth of central administrative controls transformed the loose agglomeration of feudal estates into modern countries; it required the development of central bureaucracies, which enabled the king to exert his power throughout his domain. The vital part royal bureaucracy was assigned in this process made it plausible for many of the Socialist reformers and revolutionaries at a later stage to regard the state as the powerful instrument which would enable those who controlled it to change the social system according to their ideas. The

---

[3]Eli Filip Heckscher's views (see his book *Mercantilism*, London: Allen and Unwin, 1935) as summarized by Eric Roll, *A History of Economic Thought* (New York: Prentice-Hall, 1946), p. 58.

demand for political power to enable Socialists to use the
state as an instrument of social change thus followed logically from the ideas and achievements of the mercantilists.

Once modern nations had been established, liberals, in
the sense in which middle-class philosophers and economists in
Europe used the term, aimed at the restriction of government
power. This was designed to ensure personal freedom and the
security of private property, and also to prevent, or at least
limit, the use of state power to bring about the kind of social change Socialists of the Marxian variety had in mind. The
struggle between absolutism and liberalism had reached quite
different stages in different parts of the Old World when the
labor movement made its first groping step toward self-con-
sciousness, organization, and ideology.

In England liberalism had won decisive battles when the
labor movement developed into a stable organization of some
permanency.[4] The pioneers of the movement supported the liberals in their struggle against the "Tories." Thus the early
representatives of the working class in the House of Commons
appeared under the label of *Lib-Labs*—trade unionists elected
on the Liberal party label. Some conservative leaders, especially Disraeli in England and Bismarck in Germany, made attempts to enroll labor in their struggle against the liberal
representatives of the business world. Such a conservative-
labor coalition would have caught the middle classes in a pin-
cer movement and might have delayed the progress of industrialization. Some Socialist leaders—for example, Ferdinand
Lassalle in Germany—were accused by their rivals of being
somewhat receptive to such proposals. In the main, however,
the Socialist labor leaders recognized that the precapitalistic
political forces representing the aristocracy and its allies
were as much their enemy as were the business leaders.

Still, although liberalism dominated British thinking and
policies for almost a century even when the Liberals were not
in office, it was but a brief episode in the history of the
European Continent when the labor movement was in its formative
stages. Political power thus appeared far more important an
instrument in the eyes of the workers on the Continent than
elsewhere. Continental workers expected all blessings to be

---

[4]This highly abbreviated account of necessity disregards the
local trade clubs of the eighteenth century. Formed by skilled
workers, the clubs "sought with little success, mainly by appeals to Parliament, to protect the wage standards of their
members . . . against the growingly devastating effects of unlimited competition" (Allan Flanders, "Great Britain," in *Comparative Labor Movements*, ed. Walter Galenson [New York: Prentice-Hall, 1952] p. 1).

derived in some way from their ultimate control of the state; British workers, or at least that part of the working class to whom political rights were gradually given, relied to a far greater extent on the bargaining power their skill gave them. Britain, the pioneer of industrialism, provided a comparatively high and rising standard of living for at least a part of the working class. Local self-government survived to a much larger extent than on the Continent under the onslaught of central government. The emphasis on contractual relationships in England contrasted sharply with the predominance of legal or administrative regulations on the Continent. Not until the large masses of unskilled workers entered the movement—that is, toward the end of the nineteenth century—did the British workers turn again toward the weapons of politics, and even then Marxian Socialism remained alien to them.

On the Continent the Socialist labor movement under Marx's inspiration played a key role in the struggle against absolutism and in favor of democracy. Having witnessed the decisive blows the state, with its instruments of growing power, was striking against the feudal system, the assistance the government provided to the rising industrial system, and the energy with which government power was being used again and again "to keep the workers in their place," the Socialists rejected the anarchist creed of the necessity of destroying the state. Instead, they resolved that state power was the indispensable instrument for the destruction of the existing society. Once this was achieved, they were willing to grant the anarchists that the state had outlived its usefulness and would "wither away." This, however, was a vision of a distant future. In the meantime the working class needed state power to free itself from capitalist oppression, and the royal road to the conquest of state power was democracy.

In the Marxian vision of capitalistic development, the competitive system would inevitably lead to the defeat of the small capitalist by his bigger competitor. Deprived of his capital, the victim would swell the ranks of the propertyless proletariat. Thus, as capitalistic development progressed, an increasing number of victims of exploitation would confront a smaller and smaller number of capitalists. The power of numbers would be on the side of the proletariat. Given equal right to vote, the workers would thus obtain control of the instruments of state power by their numbers—whether peacefully or by violence was of little importance. In this way the struggle for democracy and the progressive proletarization of the population would work together to guarantee the ultimate victory of the working class.

Thus while revolutionary syndicalism and Marxism joined in the rejection of the existing order of society and agreed on the objective of a classless society without private ownership

of the means of production, they disagreed on the role of political action and of the state in attaining this objective.
France, Italy, Spain, and the French-speaking parts of Switzerland were the stronghold of syndicalism, whereas the Germanic
parts of the Continent were more hospitable to the Marxian
thought. Even when toward the end of the nineteenth century,
with the organization of unskilled workers, the character of
the British labor movement changed and a political party was
established by the unions, it successfully resisted attempts
to convert it to Marxian or Syndicalist thought. Fabian socialism, which it finally adopted, was very different from
the Marxian socialism then propounded.

Three main types of labor movements thus developed. In
Britain the unions set up their own political party, mainly to
protect the collective bargaining system upon which they relied
against court interference, but also to use their political influence for the benefit of the growing number of unskilled
workers with little bargaining power who joined the movement.
In France, Italy, and Spain Syndicalists and Marxists were involved in a struggle over the role of the unions in the political field. The remainder of the Continent followed, with some
variations, the German pattern. The political party set the
tone for the movement and gave it its ideological head. However, the unions increasingly asserted themselves as equal
partners within the framework of a highly diversified labor
movement whose interests covered the entire life of the workingman.

LABOR MARKET IMPACT

Unionism played a relatively subordinate role in the beginnings of the European labor movement. The most obvious reason was the failure of unions to obtain the basic rights to
enable them to function effectively. To overcome the resistance of hostile legislation and often of antagonistic courts,
political power seemed the only means available, especially because discrimination affected all workers as a class, not simply the least skilled among them. Moreover, as long as class
solidarity prevailed and the skilled workers threw in their lot
with the unskilled, as in the struggle for political and social
equality, the rapid transfer of workers from rural to industrial occupations made unionism a weapon of doubtful effectiveness for most workers. In Britain skilled workers were given
the right to vote and to form unions by successive legislative
reforms. They responded by developing the first successful
model of "business unionism." However, when less skilled
workers entered the union movement, their relative lack of
strength on the labor market, resulting from the large supplies

of unskilled workers, quickly led to emphasis on the political means at the disposal of the workers. If nothing else, their numbers gave them influence.

On the Continent, where the expansion of equal voting rights to the workers was delayed in most countries until the beginning of this century, class solidarity proved far stronger than in Great Britain. With the exception of the Syndicalists, trade unionism, even of the higher skill groups, for a long time unquestioningly accepted the primacy of political action. The large supplies of unskilled labor coming onto the urban labor markets exceeded the power of absorption by expanding industries throughout most of the nineteenth century. For the large mass of the workers, trade union action, even when it became legally possible, held few prospects of success as long as unemployed unskilled labor was available in large supply. This situation persisted until emigration and the rate of absorption of common labor by industry came at least within striking distance of the rate with which increasing agricultural productivity or—late in the century—the cheaper imports of agricultural products from overseas released excess supplies of labor from the rural areas.[5] Only around the beginning of this century did the rapid pace of industrialization in Germany permit a corresponding expansion of effective trade unionism into the low-skill groups.[6]

Progressive expansion of unionism to lower skill groups thus had opposite effects in Britain and in Germany. In the first case it led to increased emphasis on political action in a movement that so far had put its main emphasis on trade unionism. In Germany the unionization of lower skill groups and their relative successes in union action caused the unions

---

[5]Agricultural protectionism sometimes delayed this process and thereby delayed industrialization. Modern industry had difficulties recruiting cheap labor. A case in point was that of France and its agricultural protectionism at the end of the nineteenth century.

[6]The industry share of Germany's gross national product increased from an average of 25 percent during 1855-94 to an average of 37.8 percent in 1900-1909; the share of manufacturing, mining, and construction in Sweden averaged 22.1 percent around 1890 and 31.7 percent a decade later. In France agriculture provided 41 percent of the national product in 1882; mining, manufacturing, and construction provided 32 percent. By 1908-10 the percentages had changed to 35 and 37 respectively. Simon Kuznets, "Quantitative Aspects of the Economic Growth of Nations," *Economic Development and Cultural Change* 5, no. 4 (July 1957): Supplement, appendix table 2.

to assume an increasingly important and independent role within
the labor movement.   In the end both processes led to a diversified labor movement in which political and union action were
combined and both party and unions cooperated on a footing of
greater or lesser equality.   Yet the relationships established
at the origin of the modern movements created traditions that
long influenced the thinking and the language, if not always
the actions, of the movement.

2

The Changing Nature of the Movements

With the beginning of this century, important changes in the nature of the movements—the prevailing ideologies, the structure and the internal relationships among the component parts of the movements, and their objectives—manifested themselves.

The years between 1890 and 1905 mark the high point of Marxian influence on European labor. The program adopted in Erfurt in 1891 by the German Social Democratic party, the victory of Marx's followers over the reformists, or right wingers, at the German party congress in Dresden in 1903, and the program's confirmation by the international Socialist congress in Amsterdam in 1904 were triumphs of Marxian ideas. But even during this period, opposition and cleavages within the Socialist movement appeared on the Continent, foreshadowing coming divisions. In Britain, although the Socialist idea made progress to the point that the Labour party adopted a Socialist program in 1918, the Marxian version of socialism inspired only a small sect.[1] The bulk of the Socialist movement was either of religious inspiration—of which the Independent Labour party (ILP) under Keir Hardie's leadership was the main expression—or it followed the Fabian ideas.

Fabianism—named after the Roman general whose strategy was based on avoiding open battles and wearing out the enemy—was in many ways the exact opposite of revolutionary Marxism. A small group of intellectuals, the Fabian Society, aimed at the evolutionary transformation of the capitalistic society. They rejected the labor theory of value in favor of the newly developed marginal utility theory of Stanley Jevons. The labor theory as interpreted by Marx implied that in a capitalis-

---

[1]The Marxian Social Democratic Federation set up in Great Britain by Henry Hyndman in 1881 remained a small ineffective organization. Marx himself had little sympathy for Hyndman.

tic system the worker received less than the full value of his economic contribution to output. The marginal utility theory stated that at least under competitive conditions the wage corresponded to the "marginal productivity" of labor. In the place of the class struggle as the motor of social evolution the Fabians put the rational demonstration of superior Socialist efficiency, which, they believed, would convince the population of the virtue of the Socialist system. The process of transformation would occur gradually while the modern corporation, by depersonalizing the entrepreneurial function, would tend to make private entrepreneurship less and less important. Experts acting rationally would guide society toward higher achievements in a Socialist society. The Fabian Society, founded in 1883 to propagate these ideas, attracted some of the best minds in Britain. The Webbs, George Bernard Shaw, Annie Besant, Graham Wallas, James Ramsay MacDonald, and later G.D.H. Cole were among them. Their work and their prestige gave the Fabians influence far beyond their small number.

By the turn of the century a movement away from revolutionary Marxism manifested itself in Germany, Marxism's traditional stronghold. The new movement's principal spokesman was Eduard Bernstein. His main work, published in English under the title *Evolutionary Socialism*,[2] appeared in 1899. While Karl Kautsky and other protagonists of the Marxian tradition sharply opposed him, Bernstein found the support of a galaxy of brilliant intellectuals, among them Heinrich Braun, founder of the first German scientific periodical devoted to the social sciences, Georg Bernhard, and Georg von Vollmar. Bernstein's main thesis was that capitalism was not anywhere near the catastrophic breakdown that most of the Marxians expected. Marx had correctly outlined the trend of social evolution, but he had been wrong about the timing of the events. Class conflicts had tended to become less rather than more intense, as Marx had predicted. The middle classes, whose progressive descent into the proletariat formed an essential element in Marx's system, were not in the process of disappearing. The centralization of capital failed to progress as rapidly as Marx had predicted. The power of unions was increasing, social legislation was advancing, the situation of the working classes was improving rather than deteriorating. The ethical appeal of democratic socialism rather than economic forces might be decisive. The labor movement could obtain lasting successes in a steady advance without waiting or preparing for an economic breakdown

---

[2]Original German title: *Presuppositions of Socialism and the Tasks of Social Democracy*. See also Peter Gay, *The Dilemma of Democratic Socialism; Eduard Bernstein's Challenge to Marx* (New York: Columbia University Press, 1952).

which would open up revolutionary possibilities. And Bernstein ended his attack on revolutionary Marxism in a sentence that his opponents bitterly resented: "The next steps are always the most important; the movement means everything, the final goal nothing."

Bernstein's views formed the subject of long debates in the party journals and at several party congresses. It is interesting to examine the lineup in these debates. The Social Democrats of Southern Germany—areas of fairly democratic institutions, independent peasants, and a liberal intelligentsia —supported the Revisionists, as Bernstein and his supporters were called. Northern Germany—especially the agricultural areas east of the Elbe River in Prussia with its "Junkers," its large landed estates, and conditions approaching serfdom— formed the bulwark of Karl Kautsky, August Bebel, and other orthodox Marxians. The trade union leaders sided with the latter.[3] The decisive battle was fought at the party congress of Dresden in 1903. The victory of the Marxians was confirmed by the International Socialist congress of Amsterdam in 1904, which rejected "ministerialism"—the entry of Socialists into governments of middle-class parties.[4]

Yet any objective examination of the actual evolution of the Continental labor movements in this century must lead to the conclusion that its practice followed Fabianism and Bernstein more closely than the revolutionary prescriptions of

---

[3]Similar regional differences in economic and social structure appear to have been reflected in the French division between the Marxians and the Syndicalists. See Michel Collinet, *L'Ouvrier Français: Essai sur la Condition Ouvrière, 1900-1950,* (Paris: Editions Ouvrières, 1951). In Germany the role of Prussia after 1918 was almost exactly the opposite of what it was earlier. It became one of the main bulwarks of democracy in the Weimar Republic's struggle against nazism, perhaps reflecting the rapid industrialization of Prussia.

[4]This decision referred immediately to the famous case of Alexandre Millerand, a French Socialist leader who had joined the government of Waldeck-Rousseau as minister of commerce in 1899. This step, although endorsed by the most popular French Socialist leader at that time, Jean Jaurès, was sharply criticized by the Marxian spokesman Jules Guesde. Jaurès bowed to the decision of the Amsterdam Congress, thus opening the way for the unification of the badly divided French Socialist movement. Millerand, on the other hand, ended up as a leading representative of violent French nationalism.

Marx.[5] The language retained the traditional revolutionary
terms, but the practice moved away from the prescriptions of
revolutionary Marxism. Yet until 1914 the power of the tradition and language were strong enough to prevent a full-fledged
change to a genuinely reformist policy. Until the outbreak of
World War I in 1914 the dominant current of Continental social
democracy demonstrated a strange immobility, caught as it was
between a revolutionary language and a system of organization,
a leadership, and a practical activity oriented toward gradual
change rather than revolutionary actions.

The organizational system was that of a mass party rather
than that of a revolutionary elite. Winning elections rather
than preparing for armed uprisings was the task of the organization, and the leadership was selected from the angle of parliamentary and propagandistic effectiveness instead of its
ability to lead revolutionary movements. The actual work of
the movement aimed at political, social, and economic reforms
achieved partly by legislation and administration, partly by
collective bargaining. The cleavage between language and action, ideology and reality became wider as the twentieth century advanced—until the outbreak of World War I forced the
movement to make decisions that made impossible the persistence
of the ambiguity.

THE BOLSHEVIK SPLIT

Even before World War I, a long-brewing issue had led
to what proved in the end to be a fateful division within the
ranks of the Russian Socialist movement, even though most
outside observers at the time regarded it as a tempest in a
teapot.[6] The issue was that of the role of Socialists in a
country which had barely entered upon its capitalistic stage of
development. The Marxians in Russia—who were different from
the Social-Revolutionaries (SR), a non-Marxian, peasant-based
Socialist movement—saw no way of using the still existing or
recently abolished communal property forms in the village as

---

[5]It should perhaps be pointed out that toward the end of his
life, Friedrich Engels, Marx's closest associate and collabo-
rator, in a famous article on the possibilities of disarmament
in Europe in *Neue Zeit*, came to regard violence as a weapon of
counterrevolution rather than of revolution.

[6]Rosa Luxemburg, an important figure in the German Socialist
movement although she was of Polish origin, was one of the few
contemporary observers who understood the significance of the
event.

cornerstones of a Socialist society. But when it came to the
development of their own program of action, the Marxians were
divided into two camps. The Menshevik party wing accepted the
inevitability of a long period of capitalistic development during which they would form a mass party after the German model
out of the growing proletariat that industrialization was bound
to produce. Only after long capitalistic development could the
working class dare confront the bourgeoisie. Socialism was
thus a distant goal. The Bolsheviks, led by Lenin, advocated a
two-stage strategy in which the peasantry played a key role.
In the first stage industrial workers led by the Bolsheviks
would form a coalition with the peasantry to overthrow czarism
and destroy feudal landownership. In the second stage they
would divide the peasantry and lead the landless laborers as
well as the small peasants into a revolution against the large
peasant owners and the industrial employers. The general staff
in charge of this intricate strategic maneuver would be a small
party of "professional revolutionaries" connected with the
large mass of industrial workers and peasants by trade unions
and other mass organizations, which the small Bolshevik party
would control.

Given the low level of industrial development in czarist
Russia, the Bolshevik-Menshevik split was in its beginnings not
much more than a conflict between two small sects. What gave
it historic importance was its almost accidental connection
with the much more far-reaching cleavage created by World War I.

WARTIME DIVISIONS

Throughout most of the nineteenth century the Marxian
movement regarded wars as events whose outcome could by proper
strategies be turned to the advantage of the working class.
The first change in this attitude occurred when Friedrich Engels, referring to the development of an advanced military
technology at the disposal of the ruling classes, described
violence as the tool of the oppressor rather than of the rebellious masses.[7] This change was accentuated by theoretical
discussions within the Socialist movement which concluded that
most wars in an advanced stage of capitalism—wars of national
liberation excepted—were imperialist conflicts whose issues
were of no significance to the working class. It followed that
opposition to war became a primary duty of Socialists and workers. Two questions arose: Which means should the Socialists
use to prevent the outbreak of a war and what should their policy be if war broke out nevertheless?

---

[7] In the article mentioned in note 5.

The first question was never answered by any official decision of the international labor movement. Two views confronted each other: Keir Hardie of the British Independent Labour Party and Edouard Vaillant representing one of the French Socialist currents, advocated calling a general strike when war appeared to be imminent. The Marxians asserted that if the working class was not strong enough to prevent tensions preceding the outbreak of a war from arising, the nationalist passions aroused by the outbreak of a war would weaken the war resisters even more. Moreover, resistance at that time would be more effective in countries with strong labor movements than in others, such as czarist Russia, with the result that against their own intentions the Socialists would help to bring about the victory of the most reactionary countries in which the labor movement was especially weak. This, of course, referred primarily to czarist Russia, the main enemy of all democratic and progressive movements in Europe. The decision between the opposing strategies was to come at an international Socialist congress in Vienna, called for 1914, a congress that itself fell victim to the outbreak of World War I.

A related issue was the attitude of Socialists and organized labor during a war. On that problem a decision had been taken by successive international Socialist congresses beginning in 1907. The text jointly proposed by Rosa Luxemburg, Lenin, and the Menshevik leader Martov assigned the workers a double task, once a war had broken out in spite of efforts to prevent it. They were to aim at shortening the war and to take advantage of the crisis created by the war to hasten the downfall of capitalism. This text, combined with Lenin's prescriptions about the proper form and strategy of a labor party, lay behind the split of the labor movement into Socialists and Communists that lasts to this day.

The outbreak of World War I brought the internal crises of the European labor movements to a climax. Unable to prevent the outbreak of the war, the movements divided into hostile groups. The largest, at least in the early war years, was simply patriotic, supporting its government not only to avert defeat but to achieve victory. The extreme right wing of this current was not above serving its respective government openly or in a clandestine fashion[8] and supporting imperialist war

---

[8]Thus Marcel Cachin, later a leader of the French Communist party, then an important figure in the patriotic wing of the Socialist party, is reported to have transmitted funds to Benito Mussolini to support his propaganda in favor of Italy's entry into the war on the side of the Western powers. Some German Socialist leaders were accused of maintaining close contacts with the German General Staff.

objectives. Another current defended a policy of "no annexa-
tions, no reparations"—that is, a peace of understanding without victors or vanquished. The smallest group, in which Lenin
and his associates played a leading role, aimed at the defeat
of their own respective countries in the expectation that the
destruction of the armed forces and the consequent disorganiza-
tion of the government machinery would permit the revolutionaries to take over the government. This strategy proved successful in Russia. The German troops inflicted severe defeats
on the czarist armies, which caused the overthrow of the monarchy and its replacement by a democratic regime led in its
final stages by a leader of the Social-Revolutionary party
(SR), Alexander Kerensky. This government continued the war,
in the belief that it owed support to the democratic governments of the West in their struggle against the German imperial
forces.

The continuation of the war proved to be the undoing of
the Kerensky government. Not only were the Russian armies defeated but the peasants who formed the bulk of the army expected that the new government, as the SR had always promised,
would distribute the lands of the feudal magnates and the
church among the landless peasants. Fearful of being deprived
of their share unless they were present at the distribution of
the land, the soldiers left the trenches, marched home, and in
the process destroyed the administrative machinery of the new
regime. Out of the shambles the Bolsheviks emerged victorious.
They then set up their own international organization, the
Third International, and organized affiliated parties wherever
conditions permitted. The principle to which all of these parties were committed was labeled *democratic centralism*. It provided for the subordination of all working class organizations
to the Communist party, which in turn was directed by a small
group at the top. In this way trade unions were designed to be
instruments of the party directorate.

UNION-PARTY RELATIONS

Various patterns of union-party relations prevailed in Europe throughout the nineteenth century. In most countries, as
was pointed out, unions were prohibited or were rendered ineffective in the early stages of industrialization. After this
handicap was overcome three main patterns of union-party relations emerged: the British, the Germanic, and the Romance patterns, as they may be labeled, after the area in which each
originated.

The British Pattern

In the United Kingdom, after the Chartist movement and Robert Owen's Grand National Consolidated Trades Union died down and the Combination Acts were repealed (1824), labor activity centered on craft unions, also called *New Model* unions. These were organizations of skilled workers that defended their standards by a system of friendly society benefits and by requiring high dues, which effectively restricted membership and excluded unskilled workers. The Amalgamated Society of Engineers formed in 1851 was the first centralized national organization of this type, and it set an example for other crafts. In 1868 a national federation of unions was created in the form of the Trades Union Congress (TUC), which has met annually ever since. Between 1871 and 1876 legislation was passed to establish firm foundations for trade unionism. The reform acts of 1867 and 1884 gave the vote to the majority of workers. Although two miners entered Parliament in 1874, the "new unionism" gave the political drive among the workers new impetus. "New unionism" referred to the organization of less skilled workers, which began on a massive scale with the successful strike of the London dockers in 1889. By 1900 a number of unions combined with a number of Socialist societies—ILP, Fabians, Social democratic Federation—to set up the Labor Representation Committee. This in 1906 became the British Labour party. Apart from advocating major social reforms, such as the health and unemployment insurance systems introduced in 1911, the Labour party assisted the unions in warding off the dangerous consequences the Taff Vale (1901) and the Osborne (1909) judgments could have had for the unions and the Labour party. In the first case unions were held liable for the loss inflicted upon a company by a strike. Legislation passed in 1906 removed this liability. In the Osborne case unions were forbidden to spend money for nonindustrial objectives, which would have meant cutting off union financial support for the Labour party. The Trade Union Act of 1913 remedied this by introducing the system of "contracting out"—giving a union member the right to stipulate that he did not wish to pay a contribution to the Labour party. After the unsuccessful general strike of 1926 this system was reversed by Parliament, which required that union members had to "contract in"—that is, state expressly that they wished to pay the political "levy." Party membership fell substantially. In 1945 the victorious Labour party passed legislation that reverted to the previous system of "contracting out."

The present organizational scheme of the party was laid down in 1918, the year it adopted a Socialist program asking for the "common ownership of the means of production and the best obtainable system of popular administration, and control

of each industry and service." To a large extent the party is
composed of collectively affiliated organizations, but it also
has an increasing number of individual memberships.[9] Although
in the area of collective bargaining the unions jealously guard
their independence, not only toward the Labour party but also
toward the TUC, they realize how much the party can do for them
in the area of economic policy. The strongest embodiment of
this idea may be found in the TUC's Report on Post-War Reconstruction published in 1944, which came out sharply against
free private enterprise and for "the transfer to public ownership of key industries"—a policy which clearly stressed political action. However, as will be seen in a later chapter,[10]
nationalization has lost a good deal of its attractiveness
while other issues, among them wage restraint or incomes policy, have come to the fore.

The links between the party and the unions are complex.
First, by no means all unions affiliated with the TUC are members of the party, although the majority of union members are.
A union's decision whether to join the party is taken according to the procedures laid down in the statutes of the particular union. Union contributions to the party form the bulk of
the party's income. There is a joint committee of the unions,
the party, and the party group in Parliament, which endeavors
to agree on fundamental issues. Second, unions are represented
at the Annual Conference of the Labour Party with overwhelming
voting power, especially since each union casts all of its
votes according to the majority decision of the union. On the
National Executive of the party the unions hold twelve out of
twenty-seven members. Third, there is union cooperation in the
different constituencies which nominate and elect members of
the House of Commons. Some unions with a great interest in
strong representation in the House offer special financial assistance to constituency parties if one of the union-sponsored
candidates is selected to run. The miners, who joined the Labour party quite late, had for a long time a particularly large
representation in Parliament, but lately this has declined
while the giant engineering union has expanded its representation. Another giant is the Transport and General Workers'
Union.

---

[9]In 1966, for instance, union membership in the party was 5.5
million; individual members numbered close to 800,000. Affiliation through other organizations—such as the Fabian Society—
was slightly more than 20,000. Cf. Allan Flanders, *Trade Unions* (London: Hutchinson University Library, 1968), p. 154.

[10]See chap. 9.

Although the party can hardly afford to oppose the will of the majority of the trade unions, the unions are often divided on issues that do not directly affect their vital interests, which gives the party freedom of decision. However, on trade union legislation, incomes policies, and other matters directly affecting industrial relations, the party—as the Labour government in the late sixties amply demonstrated—will only rarely oppose wishes supported by a large majority of the unions. In general, initiatives for action in the political arena originate with the party, and the unions respond, positively or negatively. Moreover, in the Parliamentary Labour party—the Labour group in Parliament—non-trade unionists predominate, usually in numbers and frequently in qualities that make for effective work. Most political decisions are taken in this body.

A substantial minority of trade union members does not support the Labour party. This situation is accepted without too much trouble except in the case of Communists or Fascists. As early as 1935 the TUC warned against the election of persons as delegates to TUC congresses who are "in any way connected" with these parties. However, as the TUC has no power over the internal workings of the unions affiliated with it, some unions—such as the Transport Workers—have acted on their own to keep Communists out of union office. In the spectacular case of the Electrical Workers' Union it took almost a decade before the Communist leadership could be removed.

Outside Britain, collective affiliation of unions with Labor or Social Democratic parties exists in Norway and Sweden, but the history of this relationship and its operation are quite different from the British. A somewhat similar system existed in Belgium before World War II, but when the movement was reestablished after the liberation of the country, unions and party set up separate organizations.

The German Pattern

In almost every respect the pattern of union-party relations in Germany, Austria, and other Continental countries has been different from the British. With the exception of the small Hirsch-Duncker unions—an attempt to introduce into Germany the pure and simple trade unionism of the type that Britain developed in the middle of the nineteenth century—unions in Germany were the creation of political parties. The largest current was that of the "free" unions—those created by Social Democrats, free of employers' and government control. In due course other political parties, especially the Catholic Center party and the German Nationalists, followed the example set by the Social Democrats. For a brief period in the 1920s the Com-

munists too set up—with little success—their own unions.
However, the "free" unions at all times represented a substantial majority of the organized workers. They were also the
first (1890) to set up a union federation under the title *Gen-
eral-Kommission*; its guiding spirit was Karl Legien.

There was no question in the early years of the union
movement that the leadership belonged to the party. No one
could hope to become a union leader if he was not a member of
the Social Democratic party. The most active part of the union
membership and practically all union officers were Social Democrats. The unions recognized that only by action in the political arena could they hope to remove the legal and social discrimination of which the workers as individuals and the unions
were the victims.

Thus, the North-German federation (predecessor of the German Reich, which was established in 1871) had adopted an Industrial Code which later was extended to the entire Reich. Although the code recognized the workers' right to organize in
unions, it limited that right to workers in manufacturing; it
allowed employers to require workers to commit themselves not
to join unions, and it contained further provisos encouraging
refusal to join unions.[11] It was thus obvious that only a
change in legislation—that is, political pressure by the workers—would permit unions to become fully effective.

The economic boom beginning in the middle of the nineties
created favorable conditions for union action. Chancellor Bismarck's attempt to win the workers over to the support of imperial Germany had led in the eighties to pioneering legislation
in the area of social security. Now the unions, taking advantage of rapid economic expansion, succeeded in making collective bargaining an effective instrument of working class action. An indication of the growing power of the unions during
the years that preceded World War I is the number of workers
covered by collective agreements. In 1907 it was estimated at
900,000; six years later the number had risen to 2 million
workers. All indications were that, but for the outbreak of
the war, growth would have continued, although perhaps at a
slightly lesser pace, given the prospects of a slowdown in economic growth. Union membership grew rapidly while growing internal divisions weakened the authority of the party. "Unions
and Social-Democracy are one," Theodor Bömelburg, the leader of
the construction workers' union, said in 1902, and a similar
statement was made in 1932 by Peter Grassmann, a member of the
executive of the union federation (ADGB) and of the Social Dem-

----

[11]Lujo Brentano characterized this state of affairs: "German
workers enjoy the right of combination, but when they make use
of it, they are punished."

ocratic group in the Reichstag. In spite of their warmth,
these statements could not conceal the fact that the unions
no longer accepted the role of junior partner of the party.
As early as 1893 the Socialist leader Wilhelm Liebknecht proclaimed:

> A working class movement with purely trade union or-
> ganization cannot reach its goal. A working class
> movement with a purely political organization cannot
> do it either. The two forms of organization are in-
> dispensable for each other.[12]

Indeed, in 1906 party and unions agreed on the Mannheim Declaration, which put party and unions on equal footing:

> The unions are indispensable for the improvement of
> the class situation of the workers in the bourgeois
> society; they are no less necessary than the Social
> Democratic Party which must carry on the struggle
> for the rise of the working class and its equality
> with the other classes of society on the political
> level. . . . The two organizations must come to a
> full understanding in their struggles and collaborate.

Party and unions, however, were only the two main pillars
of an infrastructure which has been variously described as a

----

[12]Contrast this with the situation in Sweden to the end of the
last century, which very well reflects the earlier relationship
of party dominance. Donald J. Blake ("Swedish Trade Unions and
the Social Democratic Party: The Formative Years," Reprint No.
166, [Berkeley: University of California, Institute of Industrial Relations, 1961]) writes: "Party district executives
served as central organization for union activities. It was to
them that the local unions, and to some extent even the weaker
national union, turned for counsel and support. Under these
circumstances it is scarcely surprising that the Party organizations insisted upon having a say in decisions on union matters."
     Until 1909 the constitution of the Swedish trade union
confederation, colloquially abbreviated to LO, provided for
compulsory union affiliation with the Social Democratic party.
Since then the relationship has been one of free cooperation
among equals, similar to the German situation most of the time
between, say, 1906 and 1933, the year of the Nazi victory. In
general the relationship on the Continent—France being the
main exception—has evolved from party dominance to interde-
pendence between union and party.

Socialist subculture or as a state within a state. The outstanding example was probably Austria, especially Vienna:

> The Party organization was the most efficient Europe
> had ever seen. "The miracle of Vienna" was the way
> German newspapers dubbed this Socialist organization—
> high praise indeed coming from Germans, themselves
> masters in organization. The Socialists had almost
> completely succeeded in building a world of their own
> within capitalist Austria. Once one had joined the
> party, there was no need for him to come in contact
> with the middle class world outside of business hours.
> He could live in houses built and controlled by So-
> cialist municipalities; buy whatever he needed in So-
> cialist cooperatives; spend his recreation hours in
> Socialist cultural organizations; and finally be
> buried by a Socialist-led cooperative burial group.[13]

One could add the singing, hiking, chess-playing clubs, the
Children's Friends, the Socialist Red Falcons, and the Socialist Youth, the Socialist teetotalers' society, book clubs, li-
braries, theaters, and concerts—all organized by the labor
movement for its members.[14]

Even though the Mannheim agreement was canceled by the unions when the German Social Democratic party split as a result
of internal conflicts over its attitude toward World War I, the
allegiance of the union leadership to one or the other of the
Social Democratic parties was never in doubt. "We were and are
convinced," said Theodor Leipart, shortly after the reunification of the Social Democrats, "that of all political parties,
the Social Democratic Party is the only one which defends consistently the real interests of the working people."[15] Only in
the last months of the Weimar Republic did some of the union
leaders try—in vain—to come to terms with the Nazi party in
order to save their organizations and themselves. A radical
change of the union-party relationship occurred after the fall
of the Third Reich, and it will be treated in our next chapter.

----

[13]Adolf Sturmthal, *The Tragedy of European Labor, 1918-1939*,
2d ed., (New York: Columbia University Press, 1951), pp. 195-96.

[14]See Charles A. Gulick, *Austria from Habsburg to Hitler*,
2 vols. (Berkeley: University of California Press, 1948), chap.
17; Kurt L. Shell, *The Transformation of Austrian Socialism*
(Buffalo: State University of New York, 1962), pp. 9-10.

[15]A somewhat similar relationship existed between the Christian
unions and the Catholic Center party.

The French Pattern

Union-party relations in France were determined by two
main factors: Syndicalist theory and the multiple divisions of
the Socialist party. Syndicalism was shaped largely by Pierre
Joseph Proudhon and Mikhail Bakunin, the old foes of Marx within the international labor movement. Their influence at times
was considerably greater than that of Marx, and it was especially strong in France, Italy, Switzerland, and Spain, although minor branches of the movement extended as far as Sweden, and in many respects the Russian Social Revolutionary
party was allied with the Anarcho-Syndicalists.

It is difficult to define sharply the doctrine of the
movement, which ranged over a wide variety of views from non-
violence to nihilism and individual acts of terror. Nevertheless, most Syndicalists held certain ideas in common. They
opposed capitalism and aimed at a society without private property. But their vision of the "good society" was quite different from that of Marx, at least for the period immediately
following the downfall of capitalism, and they opposed the use
of political devices—even those of a democratic society. "Do
we accept the Parliament? No. Do we accept working class representation? No. Do we accept representation in the munici-
palities? No. . . . If we ask the State to intervene to set
the workers' wage do we not recognize the State's right to
exist?" asked anarchist speakers at a congress in 1880. The
state in this view was merely a device for oppression, just as
parliamentary representation was a cover for deceit and betray-
al. "Direct action"—ranging from sabotage and boycott to the
revolutionary general strike—were the means to be employed.
Neither collective agreements nor laws were of any use.

Syndicalism led to the development of an organization of
its own: the so-called Bourses du Travail, or Labor Exchanges.
Created in 1887 in Paris, they spread rapidly to other towns
and were at the same time meeting places for the unions and
germs of a new form of labor organization—a local union federation, corresponding to an American city central. In 1892,
declaring their independence from government authority, they
formed a national federation under the guidance of Fernand
Pelloutier. In the meantime, national federations of industrial or occupational unions had been formed—for example, the
Printers Union in 1881—in which Socialist influences gradually
predominated. In 1892 a confederation of the national unions
was formed, but it was only in 1902, when the two types of organization merged, that effective cooperation manifested itself. The Confédération Générale du Travail (CGT), known by
its initials, consisted of two wings—the Syndicalist local organizations and the Marxian national federations. The internal
friction between the two ideologies was settled in 1906 by the

Charter of Amiens (the city where the congress was held), which
established the principle of the independence of the unions
from all political parties. Indeed, once the revolution was
accomplished by the unions, not only the state but also the political parties would disappear. In the meantime the unions
were to organize "outside of all political schools, all workers
conscious of the struggle which must be led to bring about the
end of the system of wage-earners and employers." Although the
union member was free to join any party he wished, he must not
"introduce into the union the opinions which he defends outside." The unions themselves were the most effective instrument of the revolution.

Marxian influence within the CGT—inspired by the propaganda of Jules Guesde—was weakened by the multiplicity of Socialist factions. French politics offered little attraction to
the workers who felt—not without justification—that politi-
cians were using them to advance their own careers. Until 1914
the CGT was thus predominantly under Syndicalist influence.
Pelloutier was followed by the Syndicalist Victor Griffuelhes
and later by Léon Jouhaux as general secretary of the CGT.

World War I ended French syndicalism. In 1899 Pelloutier,
in his famous letter to the Anarchists, had asserted:

> We are rebels at all times, men truly without God,
> without master, without fatherland, the unshakable
> foes of all moral or material despotism, whether in-
> dividual or collective, i.e., of laws and dictator-
> ship (that of the proletariat included). . . .[16]

Confronted with the outbreak of World War I, the CGT abandoned
its previous threats of a general strike to prevent a war and
turned to patriotism. Jouhaux, the leader of the CGT, accepted
the symbolic title Commissaire à la Nation. In fact, this was
the end of revolutionary syndicalism, even though some of its
symbols and, in particular, frequent references to the Charter
of Amiens, lived on.

The post-World War I history of French labor was essentially a struggle among competitive labor organizations for the
legacy of the CGT—including its name, which had become a sa-
cred symbol for many French workers. The two main rivals in
this struggle were the non-Communists, mainly of Socialist persuasion, and the newly emerging Communists. Although the first
—still led by Jouhaux—were closer to the organizational ideas
of the Syndicalists, the latter were more faithful representatives of the revolutionary spirit of Pelloutier. The right-

---

[16]Quoted in Jean Montreuil, *Histoire du Mouvement Ouvrier en
France des Origines à nos Jours* (Paris: Aubier, 1946), p. 162.

wingers continued to lead most of the larger unions, but unions in general remained elite groups of small membership and limited financial resources.

> In the case of a conflict, the national organization thus had little to offer except advice and few means of imposing discipline if it wished to do so. Strike benefits were rare. . . . The absence of strike funds compelled the unions to look for quick victories. Strikes, in order to succeed, had to be sudden without a long period of consultation and negotiations. The element of surprise was the cornerstone of French strike strategy; for, if the opponent was given due warning of an impending wage demand, he would be able to prepare himself for the conflict and prolong it. Without funds, the unions would be in no position to carry on a long strike. Surprise was vital, and only those on the spot could decide on the proper moment for launching an attack.[17]

Inevitably this strategy involved a large element of risk. Yet in the absence of the traditional revolutionary appeal of the Syndicalists, the non-Communist unions had to rely increasingly on practical results which their lack of organizational power did not often permit them to obtain. Against their wishes and tradition the non-Communists—who as the majority group had fallen heir to the name of CGT—violated the spirit of the Charter of Amiens while invoking it against the Communists. The CGT increasingly depended on the political support of the Socialists and their allies.

The internal contradictions of the Communist-led CGTU (Unitarian Trade Union Federation) set up in 1921 were no less glaring. First, they had inherited not only the reflected glory of the Russian revolution but also the support of most of the revolutionary Syndicalists who had remained loyal to their original ideas. But this coalition soon split over the issue of internal discipline. The Communists had no sympathy or tolerance for the individualistic Syndicalists and their decentralizing tendencies. Nor, second, was there any agreement on the spirit of the Charter of Amiens, in spite of attempts to cover up the fundamental disagreement with ambiguous phraseology. In the end the Syndicalists were driven out of the CGTU, which, on a modest scale, attempted to follow the Leninist principle of providing mass support for the Communist party.

---

[17]Sturmthal, "National Patterns of Union Behavior," *Journal of Political Economy* 56, no. 6 (December 1948): 517.

Both trade union movements—CGT and CGTU—stagnated until
the Popular Front movement of the thirties. The impact of the
Nazi victory in Germany on the Communist movement in the world
was at first a mixture of shock and a good deal of satisfaction; by destroying democracy, the Social Democrats, and the
free trade unions in Germany the Nazis appeared to have opened
doors to the Communists. Only gradually did Moscow and its
followers realize that the Third Reich was likely to last far
longer than they had expected and that it represented a deadly
menace to the Soviet Union. A grand coalition had to be formed
against Nazi Germany, and France, most immediately threatened
by its neighbor to the east, was to be the cornerstone of this
alliance. As a consequence, the Communists entered eagerly into a coalition with the Socialists and even with the middle-
class Radicals to form the Popular Front, which won the parliamentary elections and formed a leftist government under Socialist Léon Blum in 1936. For the first time in French history
this government paved the way to effective collective bargaining on a substantial scale. The short-lived merger of the CGT
and the CGTU (1936-39) facilitated both the victory of the Popular Front and the introduction of modern industrial relations.
It is ironic that this change resulted from political developments—quite at variance with the views of the Syndicalists.[18]
With the outbreak of World War II the merger of the two union
confederations ended. The crucial issue was Communist support
of the Soviet-Nazi pact. Thus once again political developments determined the fate of the labor movement.

WARTIME DEVELOPMENTS

Two main trends stand out in the bewildering series of
events that occurred in international labor during and immediately after the war. One was the trend toward labor unity; the
other, the gradual destruction of the non-Communist labor movements in the areas occupied by Soviet troops.

The German-Russian pact of 1939 ended trade union unity in
France and the Popular Front movements all over the world. Indeed, episodes in Occupied France hinted at Nazi-Communist cooperation. However, after the Nazi invasion of Russia in 1941

---

[18]An implied admission of this contradiction may be seen in the
decision of the merger congress of the two confederations that
the unions might temporarily cooperate with political parties
in the presence of "dangers which may threaten the civil liber-
ties or reforms in force or still to be obtained." The former
non-Communist CGT held a two-thirds majority at the unification
congress.

Communist strategy underwent another of the sudden reversals
which "democratic centralism"—that is, dictatorial leadership
by Moscow—allows. Unity of all anti-Nazi forces once again
became a major objective of Communist policy, an objective that
was reflected in the international field as well, as will be
shown in chapter 11. In France it manifested itself in the
merger in the underground movement between the CGT and Communist labor groups at a meeting in the Paris suburb of Le Perreux.

More important for the long run was the destruction of independent Socialist parties and of the trade unions associated
with them in the territories of Eastern and Central Europe,
which the Soviet troops occupied as the Nazi armies withdrew.
Under the pressure of the Occupation forces, Socialist and
trade union leaders who were willing to engage in close cooperation with Communists or Communist-controlled organizations
were appointed or "elected." At the end of this process the
Socialists were absorbed into the Communist parties, and the
unions followed the general Communist pattern of party-union
relations: the unions were placed under complete party control
and became conveyor belts transmitting party policy to the
larger working class groups organized in the unions.

3

From 1945 to the Present

The break in the evolution of the European labor movements created by the victory of fascism and nazism and by World War II was reflected in the character of the movements as they gradually took shape again after 1945. They did not set out with a precise program incorporating the lessons they had learned from the catastrophe; rather, the program was subject to subtle steady changes. Only gradually did the transformation take place which distinguishes the organizations of 1970 from those of a quarter of a century before.

However, far-reaching, although not universal, agreement existed on the need for one fundamental change: the unification of the previously ideologically divided trade union movements. This internal cleavage, it was widely held, had facilitated the victory of the totalitarian forces. Moreover, underground activity during the years of German occupation and the common experience of concentration camps had brought labor leaders with different ideological commitments together. Attempts were thus made throughout the Continent to unify the trade unions.

In France the reunification of the CGT and the Communist-led unions had occurred during the war (April 1943) at a meeting in Le Perreux. In effect, as events after the liberation of France proved, this amounted to a takeover of the united movement by the Communists. The Christian unions (CFTC) refused to join, and in 1948 the non-Communist wing of the CGT broke away to establish CGT-FO (Force Ouvrière, Workers' Strength). Fairly similar was the development in Italy, where from the beginning the unified movement was but a roof over sharply divided ideological currents. Even this system could not be maintained for long. In two successive stages the Catholics and the Social Democrats broke away to set up CISL (Confederazione Italiana dei Sindacati Liberi, "Italian Confederation of Free Unions") and UIL (Unione Italiana di Lavoro, "Italian Labor Union"), while the Communists and some left-wing Socialists remained in control of the strongest confederation,

CGIL (Confederazione Generale Italiana di Lavoro, "General Italian Labor Confederation").

Permanent unification succeeded in Germany and Austria, where the Social Democrats were in undisputed control of the bulk of the trade union movement. However, political currents continue to exist and are officially recognized in both organizations in a system of proportional representation in the leadership. Thus, the presidents of all the unions affiliated with the DGB (the German trade union confederation) are Social Democrats, as are the president and the majority of the DGB executive committee, while one of the vice-presidents represents the former Christian trade unionists. Similarly, the president of the German white-collar federation, DAG (Deutsche Angestellten Gewerkschaft), is a Social Democrat. In return, union leaders are members of all the important subcommittees of the Social Democratic party (SPD) executive board. In Austria similar relationships were established; if anything, the political factions within the unions are even more openly acknowledged. Trade union leaders are members of Parliament, and they exert considerable influence in the top Social Democratic party councils. In the (Catholic) People's party unionists play a lesser part, as they do in that party's electorate.

The power relationship among the parties within the unions is expressed by the fact that the presidents of all sixteen trade unions are Socialists, and publications and union educational institutions are overwhelmingly staffed by Socialists. In both the German and Austrian unions Socialist groups exist, and particularly in Austria, party influence in the unions appears to be stronger than union influence in the party.[1] In Germany differences between party and unions are perhaps more frequent and openly stated, but they have never reached the stage at which a real conflict appeared likely.

Yet, although everywhere in Europe the unions now assert their independence and equality of status, the real power relationship still seems to give the party a predominant role in most European countries. This is partly because political success gives a party leader more glamorous roles than union leadership provides. Young men and women of talent and ambition thus may prefer a political career to a union career. Another reason was well stated by an American observer discussing the situation in Denmark:

---

[1]Kurt L. Shell, *The Transformation of Austrian Socialism* (Albany: State University of New York, 1962), p. 64 ff. Most of the union-party disagreements are settled in small circles and are rarely known by the general public.

Perhaps the most important factor in party predominance is that it is the party and not the trade union
that is confronted with the more basic problems. The
wage decisions of the trade unions are only part of
the economic data with which the party must deal, but
the converse is not true: many party decisions are outside the range of trade union competence.[2]

Moreover, when a labor government is in office the political
leadership almost automatically assumes a predominant role and
imposes restraints of various kinds on the unions—not always
with full success and for the long run, but usually at least
with partial and temporary results. Indeed, the failure of the
party to "keep the unions in line" when the party controls the
government may become a source of weakness for the party and
eventually for the unions as well.[3]

Fundamental for the evolution of the post-World War II labor movements was also the radical change—compared to the prewar period—of the economic climate in which labor operated.
Contrary to a widespread expectation, the stagnation and depression of the thirties did not continue after World War II.
The theory of "secular stagnation"[4] found little encouragement
in the facts of the quarter of a century after the end of World
War II. Indeed, after a short period of hesitation that accompanied the reconversion of the war-oriented economies, the
growth of gross national product—the measure of overall output
of goods and services—proceeded in most Western countries at a
rate for which few, if any, parallels can be found in recorded
history. Thus, while the average annual growth rate of the
United States between 1929 and 1950 amounted to less than 3
percent, it rose to 3.6 percent between 1950 and 1964 and to
4.3 percent between 1960 and 1964. For Germany the comparable
growth rates were 1.9 percent (1929-50), 7 percent (1950-64),
and 4.8 percent (1960-64); for France, 0 percent (1929-50), 4.8
percent (1950-64), 5.4 percent (1960-64). Italy, which had a

---

[2]Walter Galenson, *The Danish System of Labor Relations* (Cambridge: Harvard University Press, 1952), pp. 45-46. The Swedish unions, however, pride themselves on the breadth of their
concern.

[3]Well-known examples may be found in recent British and Australian labor history. There the accusation that the Labour party
was dominated by the unions was used extensively by its opponents in the sixties.

[4]Alvin H. Hansen, *Full Recovery or Stagnation* (New York: W. W.
Norton & Co., 1938).

1 percent growth rate between 1929 and 1950, produced an aston-
ishing 5.8 percent between 1950 and 1964 and 5.7 percent for
1960-64. Even the United Kingdom, although far behind the Continental countries, showed an average annual growth rate of 1.6
percent during 1929-50, 3 percent during 1950-64, and 3.6 percent for 1960-64.[5]

The following data are suggestive for the period from 1965
to 1969. The data represent real annual GNP growth rates in
percent.

	1965	1966	1967	1968	1969
France	2.5	4.5	3.5	4.2	8.2
Italy	3.0	5.5	6.5	5.4	6.0
United Kingdom	2.8	1.5	1.8	3.1	2.0
United States	5.0	5.5	2.4	5.0	2.8
West Germany	5.0	2.5	-0.5	6.7	7.8

Although the picture is uneven, with Great Britain falling
far behind the major Continental powers,[6] the Continent per-
formed extraordinarily well. This situation was also expressed
in employment rates for which there are few, if any, parallels
in recorded history. The mass unemployment of the thirties was
replaced by a frantic scramble for workers. A migration of
workers set in, with employers recruiting workers as far away
as Turkey, Greece, Spain, Portugal, and Yugoslavia. The bulk
of these temporary immigrants came from Italy, which for the
first time in modern history came near to exhausting its apparently limitless labor supplies. West Germany, which absorbed
some 13 million refugees from East Germany or old German set-
tlers from Romania, Hungary, and Yugoslavia, employed addition-

---

[5]U.S. Department of Commerce, "Long-Term Economic Growth 1860-
1965" (Washington, D.C.: U.S. Government Printing Office, October 1966), part 4, table 7. Per capita growth rates would of
course be lower, in view of the population increase, but would
show little change in the contrast between the period prior to
1950 and since then. For Germany, for instance, per capita GNP
grew at an annual rate of 0.7 percent (1929-50), but at a rate
of 5.9 percent for 1950-64. For France the figures are 0.0
percent and 3.8 percent, for Italy 0.3 percent and 5.2 percent,
for the U.S. 1.7 percent and 1.9 percent, with 2.7 percent for
1960-64. All of these as well as the rates quoted in the text
above are real growth rates—price changes having been discoun-
ted as well as available data permit.

[6]The United States too did relatively poorly during the latter
half of the fifties.

al hundreds of thousands of foreign workers—close to half a
million in 1966 alone. Switzerland, with a resident population
of some 5 million, was host at one time to a million foreign
workers, who represented more than a third of its total labor
force.[7]

Inevitably this radical change of the economic environment
in which the labor movement operated affected the movement's
operations and thinking. Although a rapid return to the prewar
stagnation had been expected, prosperity, economic expansion, a
labor shortage, and growing personal incomes confronted the
movement. These conditions alone would have compelled a re-
evaluation of the movement's role and tasks in a dynamic society. Yet other important factors operated in the same direction.

Full or even overfull employment and the importation of
large numbers of foreign workers meant in most cases that native workers moved out of the least desirable jobs—as earlier
in the United States, where one new wave of immigrants followed
the other in the least attractive jobs. This added to the rise
of the native workers' income, while the emigration of surplus
labor and the remittances sent home by the workers from abroad
improved the labor market situation and the balance of payments
of the less developed parts of Europe. Conspicuous changes also occurred in the occupational structure of the labor force:
(1) the decline of the proportion of workers in the primary
sector (agriculture, fishing, forestry), mainly for the benefit
of the tertiary sector (transportation, communications, public
utilities, trade, finance, insurance, real estate, service industries, and government); (2) the rapid rise of white-collar
occupations.

The following tables illustrate both kinds of changes in
a number of Western countries (even though the data are not
fully comparable). For purposes of reference, data for the
U.S. have been added (see table 1). In every case the shift
from the primary sector, which now employs 10 percent of the
labor force or less in all but one of the countries listed, to
the tertiary (service) sector has been continuous and exceedingly strong. The secondary sector, with few exceptions, has
remained stagnant. Traditionally labor organizations have had
their strongest appeal in the secondary sector.

Second, as table 2 shows, the share of blue-collar workers
in the labor force of industrial nations has declined and,
judging by the proportions of the U.S., the most industrialized
nation, is likely to continue its decline for some time.
White-collar workers, on the other hand, have increased at a

---

[7]This proportion was then reduced by legislative measures
against *Überfremdung* (being swamped by foreigners).

rapid pace, both absolutely and relative to the total labor
force. The time seems near when in all the advanced industrial
nations the statistically typical worker will be a man or woman
sitting at a desk rather than a blue-collar worker standing
next to a conveyor belt. In the U.S. this is already the case.
     In general, blue-collar workers have been far more ready
to join labor organizations than their white-collar colleagues.
(Japan is the outstanding exception to this rule.) Nevertheless, white-collar unions throughout the Western world have
grown. As a fairly general proposition it can be suggested
that although white-collar workers in general have accepted unionization less well than manual workers, there are substantial
differences within the highly diversified social groups that
are lumped together under the term of *white-collar*. Furthermore, it seems that, with few exceptions, in the countries in
which manual workers are heavily organized, white-collar workers tend to follow their example, although they do so in lesser
proportion. More important still in the context we are consid-
ering, white-collar workers tend to be less committed to the
left of center political parties in Europe. Discussing the unhappy fate of the British Labour party after 1951, Hugh Gaitskell, one of the most brilliant, although unlucky, leaders of
the party, pointed out:

> What has caused this adverse trend? It is, I be-
> lieve, a significant change in the economic and social
> background of politics. First, there is the changing
> character of the labor force. There are fewer miners,
> more engineers; fewer farmworkers, more shop assis-
> tants; fewer manual workers, more clerical workers;
> fewer railwaymen, more research workers. Everywhere
> the balance is shifting away from heavy physical work
> and towards machine maintenance, distribution and
> staff jobs. Go to any large works in the country, as
> I happened to have done a good deal in the last couple
> of years, and you will find exactly the same story.
> It is an inevitable result of technological advance.
> But it means that the typical worker of the future is
> more likely to be a skilled man in a white overall,
> watching dials in a bright new modern factory, than a
> badly paid cotton operative working in a dark and ob-
> solete nineteenth century mill.[8]

---

[8]Quoted in Everett M. Kassalow, *Trade Unions and Industrial Relations: an International Comparison* (New York: Random House,
1969), p. 55.

Table 1.

Labor Force Shifts by Sectors in Percent of Total Labor Force

	Primary Sector	Secondary Sector	Tertiary Sector
Germany			
1907	40.2	45.7	14.1
1968	10.2	48.2	41.6
United Kingdom			
1901	9.0	47.0	44.0
1966	3.0	47.0	50.0
Italy			
1901	59.8	23.8	16.4
1968	20.7	45.5	33.8
Sweden			
1930	32.0	34.0	34.0
1968	8.0	42.0	50.0
United States			
1920	29.4	32.9	37.7
1969	4.9	32.8	62.3

Sources: For Germany, Günter Hartfiel, "Germany," in *White-Collar Trade Unions*, ed. A. Sturmthal (Urbana: University of Illinois Press, 1966), pp. 162-63, and ILO, *Yearbook of Labor Statistics* (Geneva: International Labor Organization, 1969), p. 304; for the United Kingdom, George Sayers Bain, *The Growth of White-Collar Unionism* (London: Oxford University Press, 1968), and ILO, *Yearbook*; for Italy, *Direzione della statistica generale del regno, 1905-7* and *Annuario Statistico Italiano, 1969 X*; for Sweden, T. L. Johnston, *Collective Bargaining in Sweden* (Cambridge: Harvard University Press, 1962), SOS, *Folk-och Bostadsräkningen 1965*, part 4, and ILO, *Yearbook*; for the United States, U.S. Department of Labor, Bureau of Labor Statistics; *Employment and Earnings* 17, no. 2 (August 1970).

Table 2.

Labor Force Distribution by Occupation in Percentages

		White Collar	Blue Collar
1.	Germany		
	1907	11.2	50.9
	1965	31.4	48.6
2.	United Kingdom		
	1911	18.7	74.6
	1961	35.9	59.3
3.	Sweden		
	1930	15.5	62.0
	1965	39.3	49.0
4.	United States		
	1940	32.9	36.7
	1970	47.2	35.9

Sources: For Germany, Stephanie Mücke, *Die mobile Gesellschaft Einfuhrung in die Sozialstruktur der BRD* (Stuttgart: Kohlhammer 1967), p. 141; for the United Kingdom, George Sayers Bain, *The Growth of White-Collar Unionism*, p. 12; for Sweden, Per Silenstam, *Arbets Kraftsutbedets utveckling, Sverige 1870-1965* (Stockholm, 1970); for the United States for 1940, Everett M. Kassalow, "White Collar Unionism in the U.S.," in *White Collar Trade Unions, op. cit.*, and for 1970, U.S. Department of Labor, *op. cit.*

A number of important inferences follow from this evolution. If the trade union movement is to maintain its position as an influential, dynamic force in modern industrial society, it must expand into the white-collar field at a more rapid pace than in the past. Furthermore, because employers are especially reluctant to permit the unionization of white-collar workers, whom they regard to a large extent as closer to management than to the men on the workbench, government assistance in obtaining union recognition is frequently indispensable.[9] White-collar unions are thus not opposed to political action; especially where civil servants or other government employees are permitted to unionize and to engage in some form of collective bargaining, they rely heavily on political influence and they organize in large numbers. But their influence is rarely directed toward radical social change. Indeed, as Gaitskell pointed out in the speech quoted, clause 4 in the Labour party constitution (adopted in 1918), which called for nationalization of the means of production, weakened the attractiveness of the party for many white-collar workers.

Unification efforts, prosperity, and changes in the structure of the labor force were among the main factors that shaped the profile of the labor movements after World War II. The entrance of the U.S. into world affairs, especially the influence exerted by the American labor movement, added an important element to the readjustment process. Although some (rather unhappy) contacts existed between the labor movements on the two sides of the Atlantic before the war,[10] World War II and its aftermath gave American labor an unprecedented opportunity to influence the thinking and the operations of its European colleagues. In general this influence operated in the same direction as the economic, social, and political circumstances of the post-World War II era. Above all, American influence strengthened the tendency toward a radical and permanent separation between Communists and others in the labor movement.

During the interwar period the Socialist-Communist division, which had taken an international aspect after World War I, was often regarded as temporary. Hopes for a reunification came and went, according to the rapid fluctuations in Communist strategy. They reached a high point during the brief Popular Front era that reached its climax in 1936. The German-Russian pact of 1939 destroyed the hopes for unification; the

---

[9]George Sayers Bain, "Trade Union Growth and Recognition," Research Paper 6 of the Royal Commission on Trade Unions and Employers' Associations (Donovan Commission) (London: H.M. Stationery Office, 1967), p. 99.

[10]See chap. 11.

entry of the Soviet Union into the war on the side of the Western Allies revived them. World War II, it was widely believed,
would be followed by a Socialist transformation of Europe under
the guidance of a united labor movement.

The advance of the so-called popular democracies—a polite
term to describe Communist dictatorships—under the protection
of the Red Army, which culminated in the establishment of a
Communist regime in Czechoslovakia, destroyed the illusions
about the possibilities of Socialist-Communist unity or even
close collaboration. Communism appeared not merely as a system
designed to bring about social change with dictatorial means
but also as an enemy of national independence. An alliance
with a Communist party in practice meant absorption by it, as
was the fate of all the Socialist parties in Eastern Europe.
The successful assertion of Yugoslavia's independence from Moscow's attempts at domination only served to confirm the view
that collaboration with Communist parties on terms of equality
was impossible. Step by step the Socialists came to accept the
split as permanent.

The growing realization of the gulf separating the two
parties permitted other factors—rising prosperity, full employment, the gradual opening of educational facilities for the
sons and daughters of working-class families, the decline of
social discrimination, the changing structure of the working
population, the impact of closer cooperation with American labor, and so on—to encourage a reconsideration of the ideological foundations of the Socialist parties. Because the German
Social Democratic party (SPD) served as a model for many others, its evolution during the post-World War II years can be
regarded as an example of a general trend.

There are indications that as early as the twenties the
social composition of the party membership was changing and
that the party was becoming a people's party instead of a workers' party. By 1950, in any case, fewer than 10 percent of the
delegates to the party conference were manual workers, almost
half were white-collar employees, and more than 10 percent were
professionals. In the parliamentary group of the party, manual
workers were represented in about the same proportion as among
the delegates to the party conference. More important, however, is the clear indication that the party no longer wished
to be a class party but was ready to open its doors to all social groups. In the words of the program of 1959: "The Socialdemocratic Party has grown from a party of the working class to
a party of the people."

A peculiar result of this trend has been the emergence of
a trade union group as the left wing of the party. Led by the
powerful metal workers' union, which represents almost one-
third of the DGB (German Trade Union Confederation) membership,
this current has resisted and at times slowed down the trans-

formation of the SPD (Social Democratic party) to a people's party of social reform. But the change of the structure of the working population and the rising prosperity of the workers have made the traditional language of the left wing appear at variance with the facts. As a democratic party the SPD could not hope to obtain a majority as long as it appeared primarily as a party of the manual workers; nor would it express the feelings even of most manual workers if it continued to speak of a radical social transformation as the only way to ensure higher living standards for the population. Most of the left-wing union leaders were traditionalists rather than genuine radicals; they continued to use the time-honored slogans of the movement, even though their practice bore little relationship to their words.

This ideological change of the SPD can be seen in a comparison of its basic program immediately after World War II and the ideas of the Bad Godesberg Congress (1959) and the program it adopted. During the first postwar years, when Kurt Schumacher was the party leader, he formulated the views of his party in a dramatic sentence: "We shall either succeed in making the German economy socialist and German political life democratic or we shall cease to exist as a nation."[11] By 1952, with prosperity rapidly advancing, actual nationalization proposals were limited to coal and energy, iron and steel—far less than had been nationalized in France or Britain.[12] The decisive change at the congress of 1959 was the result of prolonged deliberations in which Herbert Wehner, vice-president of the party, a former Communist who dominated party strategy, played a crucial part. It is sufficient to quote a few of the main ideas of the program to sense the profound reorientation of the party. "Democratic Socialism," the program proclaims, "has its roots in Europe in Christian ethics, in humanism, and in classic philosophy. . . ." Marx is no longer mentioned— unless the reader chooses to interpret the reference to classic philosophy as implied recognition of Marx's relationship to Hegel. Anticlericalism is abandoned. Although the state is responsible for business cycle policy, the methods to be employed are to be "indirect"; in particular, "free competition and free entrepreneurial initiative are important elements of socialdemocratic economic policy." And later: "Private property of the means of production is entitled to protection and encouragement insofar as it does not hinder the construction of a just social order." The chapter on "Steady Economic Growth"

---

[11]*Proceedings of Party Congress*, 1946, p. 37.

[12]Action program of Dortmund, 1952.

concludes with the sentence: "Competition as far as possible—planning as far as necessary."

For all practical purposes the program has thus abandoned traditional Marxian ideas and the party has transformed itself into a progressive people's party. Its "socialism" can hardly be distinguished from a reformed capitalism devoted to high employment levels, a developed social security system, and progressive taxation. Indeed, the German Social Democratic party program sounds less radical than, say, the formula of Richard Crossman, a leader of the British Labour party, for whom socialism is "a moral protest against social injustice, not an intellectual demonstration that capitalism is bound to collapse; a challenge to capitalist privilege, not a proof that those privileges must inevitably be replaced by a classless society. Keynesianism may have undermined the old-fashioned economic case for Socialism, but it has left the political and moral case for it completely unaffected."[13]

Inevitably the evolution of the Socialist parties from working class into people's parties, together with the other factors mentioned above, has compelled the unions to assume wider functions which the party no longer provides. Two other factors also influenced the move: the introduction of some planning mechanisms in a number of Western countries and the attempts to minimize the inflationary pressures arising out of long-term full employment.

Informal planning arrangements involving unions have become more frequent in most democratic countries—including even some to whom the very term *planning* is abhorrent. In some cases the practice started with World War II, in others during the long-term full employment boom beginning in the fifties. Formal arrangements have been of various kinds. In France unions participate in the operations of the official planning mechanism, although their technical competency to do so effectively is limited by their material poverty. West Germany developed the "concerted action" to which reference will be made below.

At least equally important has been the development of collective agreements concluded at the level of the confederation—the counterpart of the AFL-CIO. Such agreements with top employers' associations have become more and more frequent in France and Italy and are a regular feature of collective bargaining in Sweden and other Western countries. Because specific references to such agreements will be made in subsequent chapters on collective bargaining, it is sufficient at this point simply to point out that beginning in 1957 and occurring

---

[13]R.H.S. Crossman, *Socialism and the New Despotism*, Fabian Tract 298 (London: Fabian Society, 1956), p. 5.

with increasing frequency during the sixties, agreements on
supplementary social benefits, employment, vocational education, and so on were concluded between the confederations on
both sides in France.   In Great Britain the TUC has been re-
viewing[14] wage claims of its affiliated unions since 1965 in an
effort to avoid farther-reaching government restrictions or a
heavily deflationary economic policy.   Swedish collective bargaining is based on the principle of the "solidarity wage policy," which aims at raising the wages of the lower-paid workers'
groups more than the average.   The basic agreement is concluded
between the confederations on both sides, and LO—the trade union confederation of manual workers—must approve a strike by
an affiliated union if more than 3 percent of the union's membership are likely to be involved directly or indirectly.
Moreover, the confederations are represented on the National
Labor Market Board, which administers the policies designed to
permit a full-employment economy to function with a minimum of
inflationary pressure.

In Germany a system of "concerted action" has been developed involving the government, the unions, the employers' associations, and the central bank.   It originated in the formation of a coalition government including the SPD in December
1966.   The new minister of economics, Karl Schiller, a Social
Democrat, prepared statistical and other data as well as forecasts on which both unions and employers' associations could
base their policies.   He asked the trade union leaders to cooperate in joint deliberations regarding the policy implications
of these forecasts, with the employers' organizations and under
the sponsorship of the government.   Beginning in February 1967
these conversations occurred rather frequently, and although no
formal agreements were reached, informal understandings—in
spite of some reservations—were obtained, including one on a
medium-term public finance plan up to 1971.   The personnel representing the unions consisted of top leaders of the DGB and of
some individual unions.   Later meetings of the "concerted action" dealt more specifically with problems of incomes policy[15]
and encountered greater difficulties arriving at agreements.
In Italy too agreements at the interconfederate level have become more frequent.   As one example, we cite the agreement of
March 1969 regarding the progressive abolition of regional wage
differentials, concluded between the General Confederation of
Italian Industry and the workers' confederations.[16]

---

[14]The British expression is *vetting*.

[15]Incomes policy will be discussed in chap. 10.

[16]*International Labour Review* 100 (August 1969): 166.

There has been a tendency toward settling industrial relations at higher levels in most countries. In some cases this
has been supplemented by union attempts to operate as close to
the plant as possible. However, this countertrend has been
weakened in several of the Continental countries—especially
France and Italy but also to a considerable extent in Germany—
by the absence or weakness of the union organization in the
plant and in a few cases by the unwillingness or inability of
the workers' councils to cooperate with the unions.[17]

With some measure of oversimplification—because the distinction is mainly one of degree—we can distinguish a trend
toward the development of two different types of unions: those
in which the main emphasis of union work is on the bargaining
process and those which tend to exert their main impact at the
level of legislation and administration. American and British
unions would represent the first type; most of the Continental
European unions the second. The first group is primarily concerned with the arrangements that affect the union member directly at the work place—not only wages, but also work loads,
working conditions, seniority rights, his right to a particular
job, and so on. The second type places heavier emphasis on the
factors that determine the general economic and social conditions of the country, leaving the determination of a good deal
of the detail of industrial relations as it arises in the work
place to nonunion organizations such as the workers' council or
even to direct arrangements between union member and the enterprise. The contrast can easily be overstated. Although the
bargaining unions—as the first type may be called—put collective agreements and their administration in the center of their
activity, they rarely fail to also devote a good deal of attention to the general economic, social, and political policies
which may directly or indirectly affect the life and the working conditions of their members. But this part of their activity is clearly secondary to the collective bargaining process;[18]
they do not wish to assume managerial responsibilities. They
exert their influence from the outside, as it were, and avoid
becoming part of management, even though indirectly they tend
to affect it profoundly.

The "administrative" unions, on the other hand, although
they are mainly engaged at a level above the enterprise, increasingly show a desire to become more directly involved in
the issues that arise in the work place. The eagerness with
which the German metal workers' union has been developing a

---

[17]See chap. 8.

[18]And U.S. unions tend to apply to it even the bargaining techniques with which they are so familiar.

network of shop stewards in the plants next to the system of
workers' councils testifies to this tendency, as does the law
permitting the operation of a union section in the plant, which
the French unions obtained as a result of the great strikes in
1968.   Yet the mere existence of workers' councils—independent
in varying degrees from the union—makes it difficult for the
administrative unions to operate in the plants.   Moreover, in
many countries unions have no machinery at the plant level, although union leaders have been involved in high government affairs.   French planning, German "concerted action," and German
codetermination are indicative of this trend.[19]   A symptom of
the difference in approach may be the contrast between the German works' constitution law, which puts union representatives
on the boards of larger enterprises, and the union decision
that prohibits British union leaders from holding seats on the
boards of nationalized enterprises while serving as union officers.[20]   One is tempted to describe the difference between the
two types of unionism in terms of their center of gravity: in
bargaining unions it is far lower in the industrial relations
system than in administrative unions.

Each arrangement creates problems and has advantages and
disadvantages.   The bargaining union in the United States may
have to devise indirect means of pressure to effect changes
only legislation can bring about.[21]   British unions, although
their affiliation with the Labour party enables them to influence legislation and administration through their membership in
the party, find that as the social configuration of the British
population changes, their role within the party diminishes, and
defects in their work-place organization have allowed a competitive organization, the shop stewards, to displace them at crucial moments in the determination of effective wages and working conditions.

The bargaining unions, moreover, are forced to recognize
how much their successes and defeats depend on the general eco-

---

[19]A sense of this distinction first came to me when a French
trade unionist pointed out with pride that Léon Jouhaux, then
leader of the non-Communist FO confederation, could see the
prime minister any time he wished.   It would have been far more
difficult for him or any other union leader to see the director
general of many private enterprises.

[20]See chap. 9.

[21]Supplementary unemployment benefits in the U.S. were at least
partly designed to induce employers to use their political influence in conjunction with the unions in order to increase public unemployment benefits.

nomic policies pursued by public authorities. The problems
created by full employment make it difficult for the government to continue to regard the wage bargain as a private af-
fair of the partners to the agreement. The unions are thus
compelled to seek ways of influencing public policy, if only
in order to avert government intervention in the bargaining
process or its results.

The administrative unions discover increasingly that
their tendency to operate at high levels of public or private
decision-making cuts them off from their rank and file; the
union leaders become part of the "establishment." Some observers have discerned a paternalistic tendency in the approach
of these unions to their membership. Also, rival organizations
spring up in the plant and claim the primary loyalty of the union members.

The flaw in the system manifested itself explosively in
the wave of wildcat strikes that swept across Western Europe
in 1968 and 1969. The first and most dramatic one occurred
in France in May and June 1968. We are not concerned here with
the student rebellion and the political crisis, even though
they were essential parts of the movement, but rather with the
industrial relations crisis. Its main manifestations were the
spontaneous occupation of plants, the size of the strike movement, and the eagerness of the employers and of the authorities
to capitulate. The results of the movement were mainly the
fulfillment of demands that had long been on the agenda but
which until then the unions had little hope of achieving in the
foreseeable future: wage increases, reduction of geographic pay
differentials, reduction of hours of work, the presence of union sections in the plant. What started as a threatening revolution thus ended in a big step forward in social reform, although it was essentially a continuation of previous developments.[22]

Equally important, however, is the undeniable fact that
the unions were surprised and bypassed by the strikes—as had
been the case often before—and that all but perhaps the CFTD
(the former Christian trade unions) had great difficulties in
regaining control of the movement. The gap between the major
policy-makers at the head of the confederations and the rank
and file had been aggravated by the increasing need, created by
the pace of technological and other changes, to make important
decisions within the plant, in which the unions had little say.

The French strikes were followed in September 1969 by a
sudden wildcat strike movement that originated in the biggest

---

[22]I follow here a study by Gerard Adam, Jean-Daniel Reynaud,
and Jean-Maurice Verdier which Jean-Daniel Reynaud (Paris) has
made available to me in manuscript.

Fiat plant in Turin, Italy. The members of the union grievance committee who tried to resist encountered hostility, and the workers refused to be represented by them. Although this strike was settled within a few days, another broke out in the same plant a few weeks later, and once again the unions had difficulty regaining control of the movement. Waves of wild-cat strikes—automobile, petrochemical, and steel were hardest hit—shook the entire social structure of Italy, including the union leadership of all political persuasions. Cooperation among the ideologically split unions developed in the face of declining membership and loss of their authority. Extreme left-wing movements opposing all unions and political parties sprang up in various industrial centers.

More surprising than the explosions in France and Italy was the sudden outbreak of wildcat strikes in West Germany—a country with an exceedingly low strike frequency throughout the post-World War II period. The movements which started in September 1969 occurred during the lifetime of collective agreements—concluded for a period of eighteen months during a short-lived recession—which imposed, under German law, the duty upon the unions to maintain "social peace" for that period. The rapid capitulation of management in the first of the struck enterprises, the Hoesch metalworks, was a signal to the workers in other plants to follow suit, and the unions were compelled to raise their demands in order to regain control of the spontaneous movements.[23] This occurred at the same time that the first goverment under Social Democratic leadership in the post-World War II era was in office, which the unions did not wish to embarrass by inflationary wage demands. The alienation of the rank and file from the union leadership[24] and the readiness with which employers were willing to share their high profits with rebellious employees in an exceedingly tight labor market did not give the union leaders much choice if they wanted

---

[23]In the first quarter of 1970 seventy-five wildcat strikes occurred within the jurisdiction of the most radical of the German unions, the I. G. Metall (metalworkers' union) alone.

[24]"A constantly shrinking number of dignitaries makes the central decisions—including the compromises during collective bargaining—without drawing a larger layer of activists into the decision-making process." Quoted from an unpublished book by Eberhard Schmidt, member of the metalworkers' union, in *Der Spiegel* 24, no. 45 (November 2, 1970): p. 36. The "official" interpretation of the events—quite frank in most respects—was presented by Gerhard Leminsky in *Gewerkschaftliche Monatshefte* 20, no. 11 (November 1969). Leminsky is a research associate in the Economic Research Institute (WWI) of the DGB.

to regain control of the events. Moreover, several of the union leaders, especially Otto Brenner, the leader of the metalworkers, belong to the left wing of the SPD, which accepted
only reluctantly the "revisionist" trend of the party leadership. In the meetings of the "concerted action" in 1970 the
conflicts between the union representatives and those of the
employers' associations became increasingly sharp.

This survey of rank and file unrest in Europe, incomplete
as it is, must include a brief reference to the first major
disturbance of industrial peace in Sweden since the conclusion
of the Basic Agreement by labor and management in 1938. "The
unrest indicates the erosion of the traditional confidence in
the trade union leadership."[25] Underlying the rebellion is
dissatisfaction with the highly centralized bargaining system
introduced in Sweden in 1956. The most dramatic event was the
strike of metal mine workers above the Arctic Circle in an almost entirely government-owned enterprise in December 1969. A
sit-down strike protested against the piece work rates, the
poor working conditions, and the weak union. The strikers rejected a settlement negotiated by their union and asked that
management negotiate directly with their strike committee, bypassing the union. A revision of the entire bargaining system
may result from the event.

Although the "administrative" unions have suddenly been
forced to realize the distance between union leader and rank
and file, the problems of the "bargaining" unions, especially
in a period of full employment, are hardly less acute. Required first, however, is a brief discussion of the main bargaining systems used in Europe.

A rapid survey of union strength (as expressed in union
membership) in a number of Western countries may be helpful.
Relatively recent figures—most of them referring to 1967 or
1968—show the following picture:[26]

---

[25]Foreign Labor Briefs in U.S. Department of Labor, *Monthly
Labor Review*, May 1970, p. 68.

[26]Sources: Various union reports; London *Economist*, October 26,
1968. The figure and percentage for Italy seem unduly high.
Methods of counting members vary from country to country.

United States	16.7 million
Great Britain	10.1 million
Japan	9.4 million
Germany (West)	7.0 million
Italy	7.0 million
France	3.2 million
Sweden	2.2 million
Austria	1.5 million
Netherlands	1.2 million

The proportion of the labor force organized in unions may be more significant. The following situation emerges (the sources are the same as above):

Sweden	60 percent
Austria	47 percent
Britain	40 percent
Italy	35 percent
Netherlands	27 percent
Germany (West)	26 percent
United States	22 percent
Japan	20 percent
France	16 percent

Part Two

4

Collective Bargaining Patterns

Outside the United States and Great Britain collective bargaining has not acquired the primary importance in the industrial relations system that it has in most of the Anglo-American world. First, most nonwage conditions of employment are regulated by law. Minimum wages determined by law or administrative action have at times influenced not only the bottom of the wage structure but almost the entire wage system, because most wage rates were close to the minimum. Wage supplements, such as family allowances set by government authority, are in many countries of fundamental importance in determining family incomes. Under a variety of conditions the government may "extend" a collective agreement—that is, make all or part of it applicable to enterprises not represented at the bargaining table. Although it is an oversimplification to affirm that pure collective bargaining exists in either the United States or the United Kingdom, collective agreements are the prevailing method of the industrial relations system in these countries. The impact of collective bargaining, its pattern-setting influence, extends far beyond the immediate scope of the agreements. By contrast, such agreements play a lesser role in most, if not all, countries of the European continent. The influence of the government in all its branches and of agreements at the interconfederal level permeates large parts of the system.

An outstanding example of the powerful, historically determined trend toward legal rather than contractual regulation is the case of the extended paid vacation periods in France. When the automobile firm Renault granted a third paid vacation week to its employees in 1956, the government of Prime Minister

Guy Mollet, a Socialist, proceeded to generalize this conces-
sion by law. Renault added a fourth paid vacation week in
1962, and the extension of this to other enterprises was left
by de Gaulle to collective agreements. In 1969, however, the
post-de Gaulle regime once again "legalized" the contractual
arrangements. This trend at least partly explains the evolution of most Continental trade unions in the direction of what
we have called the "administrative" union.

Second, the power of the employers in several, although by
no means all, countries is still great enough to keep wages and
working conditions in large areas—both geographic and occupational—at their unilateral determination. This does not necessarily mean that employers exploit unorganized workers. The
labor shortages that have prevailed in many countries since
shortly after World War II have caused most employers to offer
attractive wages and working conditions, often exceeding the
rates set in collective agreements or the conditions determined
by law. Mass migration of workers from labor surplus areas to
labor shortage areas has not overcome the tendency to regard
contract terms and legal regulations as minima to be exceeded
in order to attract or retain manpower of the desired quality.

Third, collective agreements on the Continent, and often
in England as well, cover large areas and thus a number of
firms. The agreements are therefore usually brief, leaving the
often complicated details of fringe benefits, wage differentials, and so on outside their scope. Moreover, as was just
pointed out, the wage rates set in the agreements are commonly
regarded as minima upon which a pyramid of effective rates and
earnings is established by a number of arrangements. Sometimes
the workers' council, legally and in many cases also in fact
independent of the union, bargains for higher rates, supplements of various kinds, guaranteed overtime, added fringe benefits, and so on. Individual workers may make their own supplementary arrangements with management, and under the pressure of
tight labor markets, firms may offer wage supplements even
when, as was the case for a time in Holland, such "black market" wages violate the law. In these arrangements, the union
plays no part. From the point of view of management, the system of such supplementary nonunion agreements has the advantage
that these concessions have no legal validity and can be withdrawn unilaterally by the employer if the economic or labor
market situations change, as opposed to the obligations created
by the contract.

Finally, the division of unions along political or religious lines makes collective bargaining a difficult enterprise
in the face of usually unified employers' associations. The
unification of the trade union movement in a few European countries after World War II has somewhat reduced the importance of
this fact, as have new forms of cooperation among divided un-

ions such as the Foundation of Labor in the Netherlands. Yet
internal cleavages of organized labor persist in a sufficient
number of countries to affect substantially the industrial relations system of the European continent.

Because conditions vary from country to country and over
time, it is difficult to generalize. Even among the Continental countries themselves the differences are considerable. Yet
the spirit of the British and American systems is sufficiently
different from that of the Continental systems to enable us to
attempt some generalizations, even though they may have to be
qualified in many respects. In summary, we list some of the
main characteristics that distinguish collective bargaining in
most non-Socialist countries of Europe from the U.S. system.

1. Legislation and administration determine the sub-
    stance of industrial relations to a far greater
    extent than in the U.S. This statement applies
    especially to fringe benefits. Collective agree-
    ments and other arrangements mainly add supple-
    ments to legally fixed benefit minima. In this
    respect the United Kingdom has so far followed
    the U.S. pattern more closely than the continen-
    tal model.

2. Most collective bargaining in Europe is far more
    centralized than in the U.S. The typical agree-
    ment covers an industry—sometimes even groups of
    industries, as do some agreements of I. G. Metall
    in Germany—and thus covers a multitude of firms
    extending over large areas or even the entire
    country. The partners to the agreement are typi-
    cally employers' federations rather than individu-
    al establishments and a union or group of unions.
    As a consequence, the agreement does not regulate
    more than some basic facts of the employment re-
    lationship. Compared to an American agreement it
    is exceedingly brief and simple. In some coun-
    tries, especially Great Britain, a large part of
    industrial relations is regulated by custom or un-
    written understandings.

3. In some countries—especially France, Italy, and
    to some extent Sweden—some collective agreements
    are concluded even on a confederation level. It
    is as if the AFL-CIO were to conclude agreements
    with a representative organization of all or most
    nonagricultural employers. Such agreements may
    deal with supplementary fringe benefits—that is,
    going beyond the minima set by law—or with the
    total allowable wage increase. The trend toward
    such policy-making agreements seems to be quite
    strong on the Continent.

4. This bargaining system is highly centralized at
    the top levels, but there is an equally highly
    decentralized bargaining system at the work place.
    This system is operated mainly by nonunion organi-
    zations such as the workers' councils, and it is
    often outside union control. At these levels most
    of the details of industrial relations are deter-
    mined. Wage supplements, incentive pay systems,
    and piece rates are also frequently set in these
    decentralized and often informal agreements.
5. On the employers' side, normally a unified associ-
    ation with a high degree of discipline appears at
    the bargaining table; on the union side, multiple
    representation is not infrequent. The principle
    of "exclusive bargaining rights," U.S. style, is
    unknown in law and frequently not applied in prac-
    tice. Minority unions flourish and share in bar-
    gaining. Multiunion bargaining occurs in two
    forms: ideologically competitive unions or unions
    with overlapping jurisdictions. The first case
    is more frequent on the Continent, the second in
    Great Britain.
6. Work rules are rarely set out in any detail on
    the Continent, where unions only exceptionally at-
    tempt to intervene in this area of industrial re-
    lations. In Great Britain elaborate work rules
    exist—often providing for "feather-bedding"—but
    they are mainly unwritten and traditional. The
    seniority principle, to the extent to which it
    prevails at all, is equally informal and tradi-
    tional.

UNIONS AND PLANNING[1]

In the early 1960s it seemed that growing European prosperity went hand in hand with increasing social tranquility.
Strikes decreased in frequency and intensity, mechanisms had
been set up to involve trade unions in general economic and social policy-making, unemployment had not only been reduced to
rock-bottom but had given way to almost universal labor shortages, social security systems were being expanded and improved,
and fringe benefits were higher and better than ever before.
     Perhaps most characteristic of the mechanisms involving
the unions in general policy-making was the role unions played

---

[1]The special problems of incomes planning are discussed in
chap. 10.

in a number of countries in economic planning. The pattern was
set in France, where it began as a set of emergency measures
relating to a limited number of activities, partly to overcome
the devastation caused by the war and enemy occupation and
partly to avoid a return to the stagnation that had characterized the French economy during the interwar period. Gradually
the plan expanded to cover most of the economy. The method has
become known as *économie concertée*, economic policy by way of
agreement. The term refers to the participation not only of
the state but also of the large interest groups, especially the
trade associations and the unions, in the preparation of the
plan. This is done by way of the so-called Commissions de Modernization, which are planning committees for different branches of industry whose membership includes members of both trade
associations and unions in addition to civil servants and experts. The former are not completely representative of their
organizations because they cannot commit the organizations, but
they do represent the viewpoint of the bodies. The actual numbers of such representatives are of little significance because
the committees do not vote but aim at arriving at a consensus—
the characteristic of the économie concertée. Altogether some
three thousand persons are involved in the various commissions
and subcommittees or working parties they have set up for special purposes. Because there are at least four major trade union confederations, all commissions try to have at least four
trade unionists as members.

The function of the commissions is to evaluate the objectives set for their industries in the plan, to suggest modifications, and to point out the conditions and implications for
their industry of fulfillment of the plan. They are thus to
arrive at a consensus about the plan in general and the role
assigned in it to the group they represent. In a sense this
is collective bargaining about economic and fiscal policies in
general and those to be applied to different industries and
problem areas (for example, manpower) in particular.

Although the record of French planning is rather poor as
far as attainment of targets is concerned, economic growth has
proceeded at a fast pace. However, that this is the result of
"planning" is doubtful. Nor can it be demonstrated conclusive-
ly that union participation in planning has been the cause of
the decline in social unrest until 1968, if the number of
working days lost by strikes is used as a yardstick. Perhaps
the most that can be said is that such a connection is possible. In any case, the French example has stimulated similar
experiments elsewhere. In some countries more modest planning

mechanisms have been set up, also with the participation of officers of trade unions and employers' organizations.[2]

Still, serious questions have been raised regarding the
benefits French trade unions and workers have derived from
their participation in planning. On occasion they have been
excluded from commission meetings when "business secrets" were
being discussed.[3] Few unions can afford to hire the necessary
number of experts in economics, accounting, and engineering
that would enable them to participate in the deliberations on
a footing of real equality with business and government representatives. Yet the fact that the unions are represented makes
them appear, in the eyes of many of the workers and some sectors of the public, as parts of the "establishment," sharing
responsibility for decisions they had often neither the competence nor the power to influence effectively.

Special mention should be made of the somewhat informal
way of establishing a limited planning system the West German
Republic inaugurated under the name *concerted action*. Under
the chairmanship of the minister for economic affairs, representatives of the employers and the unions, other influential
groups, and experts meet frequently to establish some degree
of consensus on economic policies. After some early successes
of these attempts, divergencies of interests and views on the
proper distribution of income (and property) have tended to
increase.[4]

When planning deals with issues with which unions are intimately familiar and government power is friendly, union participation can be far more effective than it appears to have
been in France. The operations of the Swedish Labor Market
Board have been greatly influenced by the trade union representatives on the board. This agency deals with short-run policies designed to influence the labor market directly: training
programs, travel and "settling-in" allowances for workers who
move as a result of measures taken by the board, public works
programs, and in particular the special investment reserves
fund controlled by the government. By means of tax concessions, corporations are encouraged to leave part of their

---

[2]See, for instance, Ingvar Svennilson and Rune Beckman, "Long-
Term Planning in Sweden," *Skandinaviska Banken Quarterly Review*, no. 3, 1962.

[3]French business is well known for its highly expansive definition of the term *business secret*.

[4]See, for instance, Ludwig Rosenberg (former president of the
DGB), "Pläne statt Initiativen," *Der Gewerkschafter*, I. G.
Metall, May 1971, p. 167.

earned profits in that fund. These profits are "released" to
the corporations tax free when there are deflationary trends in
the economy.[5] Union influence on the board is strong, partly
because the union representatives are highly competent and are
supported by a social democratic government.

CRISIS IN INDUSTRIAL RELATIONS?

Yet, as we shall see in more detail in the following chapters, increased union participation in economic and social policy-making is not without dangers. Union leadership assumes
responsibilities, at least in the eyes of many workers, for
many decisions it influenced very little or not at all. The
distance between the level at which the decisions are made and
the rank and file increases as the union leaders appear to move
closer to the powers that control the life of the nation.
Alienation between the worker and his union seems to be an inevitable consequence. The more the union "participates" in
high-level decision-making, the more it becomes part of a bureaucratic system of social controls, which the individual
worker feels utterly unable to understand and to influence.
The combined elites—including union leadership—are in danger
of turning into a ruling coalition, or at least being so regarded by the union rank and file.

The unending series of wildcat strikes in Britain and the
fact that actual working-class leadership has often passed from
the union to shop stewards operating independently of the union
are one aspect of the resulting crisis in industrial relations.
Even more dramatic were the events of 1968-70 stretching from
France into West Germany, Italy, and as far as Sweden. In each
case a multitude of special factors was involved. Yet the in-
cidents had in common a rejection of the constitutional union
leadership. To bring the "administrative" unions into closer
contact with the factory floor would seem a major task confronting the unions of the Continent. To make the British
"bargaining" unions instruments of determining effective wages
and working conditions and not simply more or less imaginary
"minima" is the main problem the British unions have to solve.
In both cases, however, the problems involve far-reaching
changes in the entire industrial relations system, a point that
will emerge more clearly from the chapters that follow.

---

[5]Everett M. Kassalow, "White-Collar Unionism in the U.S.," in
White-Collar Trade Unions, ed. Adolf Sturmthal (Urbana: University of Illinois Press, 1966), p. 78.

5

Bargaining in the United Kingdom

Britain may justly claim to be the mother of unionism and collective bargaining. Their beginnings can be traced back to the eighteenth century, even though existing laws made it illegal for workers to combine to improve their wages and working conditions. Gradually, beginning with the repeal of the Combination Acts in 1824, the unions acquired a highly limited sphere of legal freedom. The founding of the Trades Union Congress (TUC) in 1868, changes in legislation later in the nineteenth century, and the establishment of the Labour party at the beginning of this century set the stage for the current industrial relations system in Great Britain.[1] More than 40 percent of the labor force was organized in unions in the 1960s, and collective agreements covered an even larger proportion of the labor force. Until 1971 there had been no legal regulation of bargaining comparable to the Wagner, Taft-Hartley, or Landrum-Griffin acts in the United States, yet refusals to bargain are exceptional, and public opinion, although often highly critical of union behavior, still seems to approve collective bargaining in principle.[2]

The absence of legal regulation has led to a collective bargaining system of tremendous diversity. The nature of the agreements, the size of the bargaining units, the mechanisms

---

[1] In 1910, the Board of Trade reported to Parliament that "the method of collective bargaining may be said to prevail throughout the whole of our manufacturing industries and to a very considerable extent in regard to the employment of dock and waterside labor, and of labor employed in transportation and sea fishing."

[2] However, the nationalized industries are by statute compelled to engage in collective bargaining.

available for arriving at agreements, and the procedures for settling disputes arising prior to the agreement or under the agreement vary from craft to craft and from industry to industry. One of the fundamental reasons is the tremendous variety of union organization. Of 574 unions reported in Britain in 1966, for instance, 305 had fewer than 1,000 members and together represented less than 1 percent of total union membership. At the other extreme, 18 unions had 100,000 members or more and contained more than two-thirds of total union membership. There has been a tendency toward amalgamation—between 1958 and 1966 the number of unions dropped from 675 to 574—which produced two giant unions in engineering and transport, but there is still a long way to go before a high degree of efficiency in union operations is achieved. Craft unions, industrial unions, and general unions coexist, although rarely in pure form. The "general" unions, essentially the Transport and Municipal Workers' unions, are a specifically British phenomenon, although the Teamsters and Mineworkers' District 50 provide some parallels in the United States. The general unions are in part industrial unions; thus the Transport and General Workers' Union organizes all kinds of workers in long-distance transport (apart from the railroads) but also—as a result of many mergers—organizes workers, mostly unskilled, in a long list of industries ranging from agriculture to chemicals. Similarly, the General and Municipal Workers' Union has its center among the employees of local and other public authorities but extends also into many other industries.[3]

Neither the craft nor the industrial unions are precisely what their names would indicate. Larger craft unions contain workers of lesser skills, and industrial unions often have failed to include clerical workers or some workers with highly specialized skills. Historical accidents and different labor market strategies have led unions to adopt varying organizational schemes and to change them when technologies or other factors changed.

The General Council of the TUC, with which most, but by no means all, British unions are affiliated, has repeatedly and almost since its beginnings attempted to bring some order into the diversity of organizational schemes that creates a multitude of jurisdictional conflicts. Only partial progress has been achieved. The TUC has only moral authority over the affiliated unions, and the principle of "exclusive bargaining rights," U.S. style, has never been adopted in the United Kingdom. Yet since the fifties the rule has been accepted that

---

[3]The best presentation of British collective bargaining is in Allan Flanders, *Trade Unions* (London: Hutchinson University Library, 1968).

when a union has established majority membership in a particular establishment, no other union should engage in recruiting members in that establishment without the first union's consent. The main advance in simplifying union structure, however, has resulted from a process of amalgamation that has led to the creation of some giant unions in engineering, road transport, and a few other industries. Thus the Transport and General Workers' Union reported a membership of almost a million and a half in 1966; the Engineering Union—after its merger with the Foundry Workers—had more than 1.1 million members, and other union mergers are under consideration and may be concluded by the time this volume is published. Some smaller unions—such as two unions in the printing field—also participated in the merger movement encouraged by legislation enacted in 1964. Thus the number of unions affiliated with the TUC declined from 185 in 1958 to 160 ten years later, whereas total TUC membership increased from 8.3 million to 8.7 million in the same period. Yet the problem of a multitude of small or even tiny unions persists, and with it the number of disputes over jurisdiction that plague the British industrial scene. Further mergers would help reduce the problems created by the existence of a multitude of unions in the same plant.[4] (Britain had some 160 unions affiliated with the TUC and altogether 574 unions; in contrast, the German DGB consists of sixteen affiliated unions, with only a small number of unaffiliated unions.)

The diversity of collective bargaining systems corresponds to this variety of union structures. Because voluntarism is the basic principle, little legislation existed until recently in the industrial relations field. However, there are some important exceptions to this principle, one of which is the process of wage determination by way of wage boards. They go back to the Trade Boards Act of 1909, a first attempt to regulate wages rather than to let them be determined by contract or market forces. That hours of work and other working conditions could be regulated by law had long been accepted. However, intervention in wage setting came late and at first in a highly limited way. About half a million workers in the so-called sweated trades found their wages set by such boards, eight of which were set up before 1914. Four years later new legislation shifted the criterion for the creation of such boards from excessively low wages to the absence of adequate voluntary organization. The minister appointed representatives of employ-

---

[4]One of the reasons the Foundry Workers' Union merged with the Amalgamated Engineering Union was that the latter organized several thousand foundry workers. Another 30,000 were reported to be scattered among ten other unions. London *Economist*, October 26, 1968.

ers and workers in the particular trade, together with three
independent members. Despite the legalistic approach, the procedure in fact did not differ too much from collective bargaining, although the minister had to approve the boards' recommendations before they became binding. Further strengthening of
the system occurred during World War II, when Ernest Bevin (as
minister of labor) not only changed the name of the boards to
wage councils but also gave them the right to set "minimum re-
muneration" rather than simply wage rates. Retail trade and
the hotel and restaurant ("catering") industries were the main
beneficiaries of the change.

Of quite a different nature were the restrictions on collective bargaining imposed during World War II. The Conditions
of Employment and National Arbitration Order (1305), enacted in
1940, compelled employers to observe at least the terms of collective agreements of the industry in the district of the employer. The unions could sue employers who failed to live up
to this obligation. In exchange, the unions accepted a prohibition of strikes unless the minister to whom the dispute was
reported failed to intervene within three weeks. Voluntary
arbitration, which had long existed in many industries, was not
to be replaced but to be supplemented where it failed to exist
by this compulsory system. Thus the industrial courts set up
in 1919 to arbitrate disputes by agreement of the two sides
continued to function, but where none existed, a National Arbitration Tribunal was to decide disputes.

Order 1305 never really prevented strikes from taking
place, and a large number—mostly local and brief—did indeed
occur. Few attempts were made to enforce the order. When in
1950 leaders of a gas strike in North London were brought before the court, a resolution against Order 1305 found strong
support at the Trades Union Congress of that year. The following year Order 1305 was replaced by the Industrial Disputes
Order (1376), which abandoned legal sanctions against strikes
and lockouts but retained some provisions for compulsory arbitration. This order was canceled in 1958 under employers'
pressure—they complained that in fact it was enforced only
against them—and was replaced in 1959 by the Terms and Conditions of Employment Act, which gives the industrial court the
power to make compulsory awards in cases—brought by employers
or unions—in which a particular employer fails to observe
agreements or awards applicable to his industry. In a sense
this represented a way of extending agreements to unorganized
plants.

Later developments were overshadowed by the problems of
administering an incomes policy, a topic that will be discussed
at a later stage. At this point it will suffice to point out
the seriousness with which the British public and the government view the strike problem and the entire industrial rela-

tions system. One expression of this growing concern was the
setting up of the so-called Donovan Commission[5] to review the
problems and to propose reforms.

One of the most significant findings of this investigation
was that Britain had not one but two industrial relations systems and, further, that they were often in conflict with each
other. The formal system is based on industry-wide collective
agreements; the informal system is derived from understandings
on the factory floor between management and individual work-
place groups. "The central defect," according to the report,
is "the disorder in factory and workshop relations and pay
structures promoted by the conflict between the formal and the
informal systems." This conflict expresses itself in a gap between contract and effective wages, in chaotic forms of grievance handling, and in a disturbing number of "unofficial
strikes."[6] Part of this picture is a decline in union authority matched by a—perhaps somewhat lesser—deterioration of the
authority of employers' associations.

The gap between contract and effective rates (and earnings) is the British variant of the wider problem of wages
drift,[7] but the unofficial strike as an almost permanent phenomenon is peculiarly British.[8] However, the two problems cannot be entirely separated, because the disorder in workshop relations and pay structures resulting from the operations of the
informal industrial relations system is one of the causes of

---

[5]Named after its chairman, Lord Donovan.

[6]There has been considerable debate in Great Britain as to
whether the country is indeed more strike-prone than other
Western nations. Although differences in the definition of
strikes to be counted make an exact comparison from country to
country difficult, it does appear that strike frequency is increasing in the United Kingdom (excluding mining), that it has
been high by comparison with many other industrial nations, and
that strikes overwhelmingly have been "unofficial" (W.E.J. Mc-
Carthy, "The Nature of Britain's Strike Problem," *British Journal of Industrial Relations* 8, no. 2 [July 1970]: 224-36). It
is perhaps not simply a question of strike frequency in general, but rather one of the concentration of strikes in industries where stoppages have considerable impact on the balance
of payments or disproportionately inconvenience the public.
Moreover, the unpredictability of unofficial strikes makes them
especially hard to bear.

[7]To be discussed in chap. 10.

[8]Some 95 percent of all reported work stoppages are unofficial.

unofficial strikes. One of the remedies recommended in the report is a shift from industry-wide to plant or company agreements, which can set realistic pay rates and rate structures and more practical grievance procedures and can deal in detail with the particular problems of a given bargaining unit.[9] Industry-wide agreements should be limited to matters they can effectively regulate or should set guidelines for plant or company agreements. Most of these and other reform proposals are addressed to both unions and management.

The proposals tend to strengthen the shop stewards' position but also to integrate them more fully into the system. The proposals were also designed to overcome the difficulties an earlier distinction between bargaining and consultation had encountered. Bargaining was regarded as a union function and was to deal with interest conflicts; consultation was to be a task of the shop stewards and was to be concerned with matters on which interests allegedly coincided.[10] This, one of the fundamental assumptions underlying early post-World War II reforms, had been revealed as an illusion. In most plants consultation either never materialized or died an early death. Where it survived, it served primarily as a forum for informal bargaining.[11] Indeed, consultation became one of the mainsprings of work-place bargaining—the informal industrial relations system. Management, ill equipped to play its part because traditionally industrial relations were left to the discretion of employers' associations, and pressed by labor shortages, capitulated rather easily. "The rise of systematic overtime on a large scale, the increasing demoralization of incentive pay systems, chaotic wage relationships, growing indiscipline and, not least, an increase in restrictive practices were some of the, by now familiar, consequences."[12]

In response to this state of affairs, a trend toward "productivity bargaining" developed. In fact, trading "restrictive practices" for improvements in wages and working conditions had been fairly common for quite some time. What is new in recent British practice (as well as in the U.S.) is the systematic and large-scale development of this practice, which in Britain occurred largely under the pressure of government restrictions on

---

[9]Compare this with the attempts to conclude bargains "closer to the shop" in Germany, discussed below.

[10]Hugh A. Clegg, *A New Approach to Industrial Democracy* (Oxford: Basil Blackwell, 1960).

[11]Cf. Flanders, *Trade Unions*, p. 141.

[12]Ibid., p. 142.

wage increases. A further reference to this will be made in the discussion of incomes policies.

To return to the Donovan report, government intervention was to be limited mainly to setting up an Industrial Relations Commission, which was to examine problems referred to it by the government, to carry out investigations, and to make recommendations without legal enforcement powers, and to set up an independent review board to protect the rights of individual workers against both employers and unions. A government document titled "In Place of Strife" endorsed many of the commission proposals and suggestions. However, legislation proposed by the government went further than the report and provided for government intervention in unofficial strikes by way of a "cooling-off period," for secret ballots preceding strikes, and other restrictions. This proposed legislation ran into sharp opposition from the TUC and the Confederation of British Industry which in the end proved too strong for the Labour government to overcome. After a series of government concessions to the opposition, an apparent compromise was worked out in which the TUC undertook to examine and evaluate trade union demands in a kind of self-censorship while the government withdrew its legislative proposals. This solution left unsettled the question of the means by which the TUC could enforce its evaluation against a recalcitrant union, especially one of its giant affiliates. Even more unclear was the issue of TUC action in the case of wildcat strikes. The ultimate sanction of the TUC would be to suspend or expel a union; it appeared doubtful whether such sanctions would be taken frequently or would prove effective in restraining unions or shop stewards; the public was left in the dark about what action the TUC could take against nonaffiliated unions. Further legislation on industrial relations was to be introduced in due course, and the Industrial Relations Commission was set up by decree. Its chairman was the former TUC general secretary, George Woodcock, whose place in the TUC was taken by Victor Feather.

Although the political difficulties of reshaping the British industrial relations system are obvious, it is doubtful whether the public discussion has been balanced and has focused on all the problems of significance for the country. Some fundamental problems relate to incomes policy and will be discussed elsewhere in this book. The difference between the formal and informal industrial relations systems and the issue of unofficial strikes are undoubtedly important, but they may require contradictory treatments: the first calls for a decentralized bargaining system, the second for enhanced central union authority over members and shop stewards. Although both the Donovan report and the legislative proposals devoted their main attention to bargaining structures and procedures, they also recognized radical shortcomings in some results of the

bargaining process, such as the failure of the wage structure
to offer adequate incentives for training for higher skills.[13]
Overmanning and restrictive work practices are facilitated by
the extreme fragmentation of British craft unionism. Bargaining systems and efficient use of manpower are closely related.
These problems, although perhaps the most important in the long
run from the point of view of industrial efficiency, have been
relatively neglected in the public discussion in favor of more
spectacular issues such as unofficial strikes. Legal regulation was emphasized, as opposed to the commission's primary re-
liance on persuasion and self-discipline.

The return of a Conservative government in 1970 led to a
revision of the plan. An industrial relations bill proposed by
the new government—which abandoned the Prices and Incomes
Board set up by the Labour government to regulate price and
wage increases—aroused strong protest from the unions. The
bill set up a whole series of new institutions and introduced
new concepts, the most important of which is that of "unfair
industrial practices" and the right to belong (or not to belong) to a union. Specific provisions of the bill include the
following:

1. A National Industrial Relations Court (NIRC) will
    hear collective cases involving unfair industrial
    practices and will have the authority to restrain
    strikes which might seriously endanger the na-
    tional health, security, or economy. In such
    cases a cooling-off period of up to sixty days
    might be ordered, during which all official or
    unofficial support of that strike would have to
    be suspended. In all other cases strikes called
    according to union rules will continue to be pro-
    tected against liability for damages arising out
    of the strike—the rule established as a conse-
    quence of the Taff-Vale decision. Strikes called
    by union officials or shop stewards in violation
    of union rules or of collective agreements will
    call for compensation of damages. Collective
    agreements become legally enforceable contracts.
2. Industrial tribunals will deal with individual
    grievances, dismissals, the right to belong to a
    union, and so on.

---

[13]See Guy Routh, *Occupation and Pay in Great Britain, 1906-1960*
(Cambridge: Cambridge University Press, 1965); Lloyd Ulman,
"Collective Bargaining and Industrial Efficiency," in *Britain's
Economic Prospects*, ed. Richard E. Caves et al. (Washington,
D.C.: Brookings Institution, 1968).

3. A Commission on Industrial Relations (CIR)—completely redesigned from the one set up by the Labour government—is to deal with issues such as the determination of appropriate bargaining units and the designation of bargaining agents.
4. Agency shops can be set up either by way of a collective agreement or as a result of a ballot organized by the NIRC at the request of the union or the employer. Conscientious objectors may be freed from the obligation of paying dues to the union by paying an equivalent amount to a charity.
5. A pillar of the bill is the registration of unions to ensure that unions are democratically administered. Only registered unions may enjoy the privileges the act provides, one of which is a legally set maximum for fines against unions for "unfair industrial practices." Unregistered unions may be fined larger amounts—the law provides no limits.
6. A Code of Industrial Relations Practice is to be elaborated, especially as regards information to be provided for bargaining purposes.

Although there is little in the bill itself that would appear to be fundamentally objectionable—in spite of the violent protest of the unions—only practical use can decide what it really contains. The main question that arises at this time is that, although there are many worthwhile reforms in the act, it is not clear how the act will remedy the difficulties of the existing industrial relations system in the United Kingdom. There seems to be little in the legislation that will effectively deal with the "dual" industrial relations system—the disparity between the formal agreement and the informal practice—to which the Donovan Commission pointed as the main problem to be solved.

6

The German Pattern

German unionism is historically a product of political
parties—almost the exact reverse of the British situation.
Unions were created by men whose primary interests far exceeded
the narrow boundaries of wage levels and working conditions.
Apart from a small group committed to liberal philosophies—the
so-called Hirsch-Duncker unions in the fifties and sixties of
the last century—Socialists of different persuasions were the
main sponsors of the rising trade union movement. When the two
hostile factions of the Socialists, the followers of Ferdinand
Lassalle and those of Karl Marx, merged in 1875 at the Gotha
Congress, they set the tone for the most important trade union
movement in Germany, the "free" unions. In 1890 the unions
formed a national federation whose leader, Carl Legien, was a
Social Democrat. Other parties set up rival trade unions: the
Catholics, the Nationalist party, and—for a brief period—the
Communists. Until 1933 German unionism was thus deeply divided, with the Socialists heading the strongest organization. In
the early stages of the Weimar Republic, which established the
first democratic system in Germany, the Socialist-led unions
represented 7.9 million workers—close to three-qiarters of total trade union membership—and the Christian unions slightly
more than a million.

During the first period in the life of German unionism, up
to the end of World War I, political ideologies determined the
main currents of German unionism. Political, educational, and
general social objectives—universal equal suffrage, broader
access to educational opportunities, the struggle against social discrimination—were in the foreground of the organized
workers' attention. Union leaders themselves spoke of the unions as "recruiting schools for the party." Yet with the rapid
economic expansion of Germany that began in the middle of the
1890s, collective bargaining played an increasingly important
role in the activities of the labor movement. The main successes of bargaining came in the skilled crafts, which formed the

core of the movement and produced a large part of its leadership—both in the unions and the party. The growing prosperity of the German workers contrasted sharply with their political and social inferiority in Prussia, the most populous and politically dominant part of the Reich. The revolution of 1918 at last brought political equality for the workers. Yet hardly had the Weimar Republic started democratizing the country when first inflation and then the great depression and with it the rise of the Nazi party ended the first German experience of a democratic system. Collective bargaining too, came to an end under the Nazi dictatorship; between 1933 and 1945 wages and working conditions were determined by the Nazi regime—directly or indirectly—in authoritarian fashion.

After the Nazi period the German unions were rapidly rebuilt. Three new factors entered the picture: the impact of the occupation forces, the urge for trade union unity, and the need for the development of a program appropriate for a united movement.

All occupation forces attempted to shape the reemerging movement according to their ideological and other interests, but the Soviet forces were the only ones to be successful over the long run. In the Soviet-occupied Eastern zone, all parties except the Communist party were either reduced to the status of shadow parties—not genuinely aspiring to political power—or eliminated. The latter was the fate of the Social Democrats, who were compelled to merge with the Communists. The unions followed the example of all labor movements in Communist-dominated areas—that is, they were subordinated to the party and were assigned functions according to the changing economic situation of the country and the ideological developments within the party.

The attempt to extend the influence of the Eastern-zone unions into West Berlin and the Western-occupied territory failed. A separate trade union movement developed in Western Germany under the leadship of Hans Boeckler and gradually expanded from the British zone to all three Western occupation zones and West Berlin. Finally, a West German federation of sixteen industrial unions, DGB (Deutscher Gewerkschaftsbund), was established in October 1949. The overwhelming majority of the unionized workers agreed from the beginning of the reconstruction of the labor movement in 1945 that a unified trade union movement should be created. The former ideological divisions were regarded as having paved the way for Hitler's ascent to power. Yet, reflecting the political orientation of its leadership and even more of the most active part of its membership, the DGB is led by Social Democrats, with members of the trade union wing of the Christian Democratic Union (CDU) form-

ing the main minority.[1]   A small Christian federation, with its
main strength in the Saar district, is the only survivor of the
ideological split of the pre-Hitler era.   A separate white-collar federation and a civil servant federation represent different occupational groups.[2]   Each industrial union is represented
on the executive of the DGB, which has in addition a full-time
board of its own.   Union dues are fairly high and are paid
regularly; the unions have substantial funds at their disposal.

German industrial relations are fundamentally affected by
the organizational structure of the unions.   The lowest level
of the union is typically a local organization covering a number of enterprises.   The union is hardly involved in the industrial relations of a single plant, which are the domain of the
workers' council.[3]   The union operates primarily at the national or regional industry level by collective agreements or by
influencing government policy on economic, social, and occasionally political issues.   The typical collective agreement is
concluded between a union and an employers' federation and covers a multitude of plants over a large territory.   There are
typically two kinds of agreements: (1) a master agreement (*Man-
teltarif*), which may cover the entire branch of an industry in
the country, determines overall conditions, and may last several years; (2) a wage agreement (*Lohntarif*) within the framework
of the master agreement, which usually covers smaller territories and may be renegotiated every year.   Because these agreements cannot take into account the great variety of situations
in different plants, they are usually brief and simple.   Moreover, a large part of industrial relations is regulated by laws
and decrees of public authorities.   As a result, contracts are
often limited to determining one or two basic wage rates and
minimal working conditions.   Frequently these are set close to
the levels acceptable to the least efficient enterprises.   On
the basis of the contracts, more or less formal plant agreements with the workers' council or individual arrangements are
concluded which determine the actual rates of pay.   As a result, a gap exists at almost all times between the actual rates
described in the contracts.   In periods of tight labor markets

---

[1]The Communist party has been declared illegal throughout most
of the post-World War II era in West Germany.

[2]However, large numbers of white-collar workers belong to the
industrial unions of the DGB.

[3]Under the law the council is not a union organization, although in many cases union officers or members are elected to
the councils, and unions make strenuous efforts to maintain
close contact with them.

the gap may become so wide that changes in contract rates may
have little or no influence on the effective pay rates of many
or even most workers. This is one basic form of what has come
to be known as *wages drift*.[4] Union contract policy then becomes a highly inefficient and indirect instrument to influence
effective rates and earnings. Yet there is an important distinction between contract rates and those set in other ways:
the first are legally enforceable, the second are not. A short
but sharp recession in 1967 caused some employers to reduce or
eliminate wage elements that were not set in agreements with
unions. However, the incident was too brief to leave a lasting
impact on the bargaining system. A crisis of a different kind
arose shortly afterward.

In the course of 1969 a series of wildcat strikes occurred
for the first time in many years. They started in a few steel
plants in the Ruhr and spread to steel and coal in the Saar
district and to shipyards in Hamburg and Kiel. At times some
70,000 workers were involved. The strikes expressed the dissatisfaction of the workers with the failure of their earnings
to rise in line with the high prosperity of German industry.
So great was the shock of German management that it capitulated
in almost all cases to this surprising manifestation of workers' dissatisfaction and offered wage increases from 10 to 14
percent. It may thus be fairly said that the German collective
bargaining system responded only sluggishly to the economic
situation, but that its shortcomings—if such a slow response
is a shortcoming—emerged clearly only in the recent past.

To some extent this "explosion" of unrest expressed rank
and file feelings that union participation in "concerted action"—high-level understandings on the limits of union wage
demands and price increases—has hampered labor action far
more than the price and profit policies of the enterprises.
Moreover, as contracts usually include a "no strike" clause and
are legally enforceable, the unions were unable to respond to
the rapid change of the business situation after the recession
of 1967. In the end the unions regained control of the strike
movement, however.

A number of unions have recognized the problems involved
in this bargaining system and have attempted to establish a
contract system "close to the plant." This term indicates the
wish to conclude contracts with individual firms or smaller
groups of firms so that wages can be adjusted to the possibilities of the particular enterprise rather than be treated as a

---

[4]Other forms—which may or may not be concurrent with the one
mentioned above—are the introduction of supplements and bonus-
es during the life of the contract or the setting of very loose
piece rates.

minimum. Employers have so far resisted these attempts, which might weaken their solidarity. A significant incident of this kind occurred in the rubber industry in 1970 and ended in the defeat of the union.

Agreements concluded with firms that employ more than half the labor force of a given industry in the area to which the agreement applies may be "extended" by government authority. This gives them the force of law and makes the agreement binding on all firms of that industry and area. The interesting point is that extension depends on the membership of the employers' association rather than of the union, which gives greater incentive to the recruitment of members for the first than for the labor organization. This is one of several factors that might explain the relatively low and stagnant union membership—about 27 percent of the labor force and declining as a proportion.

If the agreement is not extended, its obligations are limited to the firms that are members of the employers' federation. This, in combination with the commitment to industrial peace which signatories to an agreement accept, produced an interesting situation in 1963. The German subsidiary of Ford did not belong to the employers' association. The metalworkers' union called a strike against Ford because it refused to enter into an enterprise agreement proposed by the union. Ford hastily joined the employers' federation, thereby accepting the agreement signed by the federation, but making it legally impossible for the union to call a strike.[5]

CODETERMINATION

Next to the distance between contract and effective rates, the system of workers' participation in management has been the most significant factor in German industrial relations since World War II. It consists of two elements: institutions created by the Works' Constitution Act covering all German industry and the special codetermination system applying only to coal and steel.

Historically the first can be traced back to World War I, when the imperial German government offered legislation protecting elected employee representatives within the plant against discrimination and dismissal. In exchange the unions committed themselves to abstain from strikes for the duration of the war. Although some trade union leaders opposed a system

---

[5]Hans Reichel, "Recent Trends in Collective Bargaining in the Federal Republic of Germany," *International Labour Review*, vol. 104, No. 6, Dec. 1971, pp. 469-87.

which gave non-trade unionists an equal voice in the selection
of the workers' spokesmen, the great majority welcomed the
protection the law offered to the trade union representatives
who might be victorious in the plant elections. Once created,
the institution of the workers' councils became firmly established among the workers. This was shown by the fact that upon
the withdrawal of German troops toward the end of World War II,
workers in Germany proceeded spontaneously to elect new workers' council members. Yet the councils have created numerous
problems for the unions.

The main functions of the councils have been redefined in
post-World War II legislation, the Works' Constitution Act,
which applies to all private enterprises. The council is elected by all employees, whether union members or not, supervises
the observation of contract clauses, and serves as an instrument of workers' participation in management.[6] Separate elections take place for manual and white-collar employees. The
council has the right to join in the decision-making process on
questions affecting working conditions; it may intervene in
group dismissals and transfers by appealing to the labor court
and in individual grievance cases by consulting with management. It administers the welfare institutions of the plant.
Beyond that, an economic council representing both the workers'
council and management is entitled to information about the
business—insofar as no "business secrets" are involved. Finally, the council is represented on the supervisory boards of
share companies by one-third of the board members. It is perhaps not unfair to point out that neither the information
clause nor the board representation has proven of great importance for the employees, whereas the influence of the council
on matters affecting working conditions and layoffs has been
very useful.

For coal and steel, special legislation—the so-called
Codetermination Law—provides two additional features beyond
those contained in the Works' Constitution Act. The supervisory boards of the coal and steel companies consist of an equal
number of representatives of the shareholders and of the employees, plus an additional "neutral" member, normally elected
by both sides. The worker members are partly employees of the
firm, partly trade union representatives. In addition, one
member of the board of management, usually nominated or at
least agreed to by the trade union—the labor director—deals
with industrial relations. It is not difficult to see in codetermination a program on which Social Democrats and Christian

---

[6]As such the council cannot call strikes or take other measures
of combat against the employer.

unionists, now united in a single union federation, could cooperate.

Union representation in management is thus strongest in the coal and steel industries, but the unions are attempting to extend this codetermination scheme to other industries. Union influence under this scheme operates most directly at high managerial levels, as it does in collective bargaining by way of employers' associations. The defense of the individual workers' everyday interests is still in the hands of the workers' council, basically a nonunion body ill-equipped for the task because it is an institution of cooperation rather than combat. German unions thus represent another example of "administrative" unions. One result of this evolution has been a declining interest of the workers in both councils and unions—the councils because they can argue but not fight and have sometimes tended to become associated with management, the unions because they operate above the plant level and thus often outside the scope of the workers' immediate daily interests.[7] It should be pointed out that some of the unions are increasingly aware of these problems and are trying to establish themselves in the plants by way of shop stewards, who are to work with and through the councils. However, the close association of some of the councils with management has led occasionally to considerable strains in the relation between councils and unions.[8]

The system of codetermination in coal and steel has been the object of a good deal of critical examination, especially by American observers. Their doubts refer mainly to the double

---

[7]As one piece of evidence, in 1957 in North Rhine-Westphalia, the industrial heart of West Germany, only 40 percent of the eligible enterprises held elections for workers' councils. In 1961 in a large industrial city over one-third of all enterprises employing 100 to 200 employees did not have a workers' council. See Friedrich Fürstenberg, "Workers' Participation in Management in the Federal Republic of Germany," *Bulletin of the International Institute for Labour Studies* 6 (June 1969): 105, 112 ff. Evidence for the declining attractiveness of the unions is the rapid membership turnover and the fact that union membership represents a declining proportion of the labor force.

[8]German trade unionists often complain of the councils' "shop selfishness" (*Betriebsegoismus*) when councils take advantage of a specially favorable situation to obtain additional benefits for the workers of a given plant. The system of multiplant bargains makes it difficult to use advances in one enterprise as levers for generalized progress.

role of unions under the system—they are at the same time part
of management and representatives of the employees. This applies also to the labor director, who is not only nominated by
the union but in the majority of cases started out as a blue-
collar or white-collar worker; two-thirds of the labor directors have no more than primary school education.[9] The problem
of labor directors gaining the acceptance of management without
at the same time losing contact with the employees has its
roots in the need for a compromise between the conflicting demands of the enterprise and those of its employees. Although
most directors regard the interests of the enterprise as their
overriding concern, they have undoubtedly helped to make more
tolerable for the workers the difficult adjustment processes in
the declining coal industry.

The German unions are striving for the extension of the
codetermination scheme of the coal and steel industries to all
industrial enterprises of a specified size.[10] Whether they
will succeed in this effort depends primarily on the internal
political evolution of West Germany. However, for many workers union activity above the plant level or the issue of union
representation at higher managerial levels has little immediate
relevance. The events of 1969 testified to considerable es-
trangement between rank and file and union leadership, including and perhaps even especially in the codetermination industries.

Considerable impetus was given to the union demand for the
extension of codetermination by an expert commission appointed
by the government to report on the functioning of codetermination, the Biedenkopf Commission (after the name of its chairman). The report of this commission (made public in 1970) generally endorsed the principle of codetermination, and recommended its extension but suggested that stockholders retain a
majority of the seats on the supervisory boards. To give the
unions equal representation would substitute compromises in the
supervisory board for open social conflict and thus would en-
danger trade unionism itself. Nor was there any need, in the
view of the commission, for the labor director to be appointed
in any different fashion from the other directors—that is,
with special union approval—because he could hardly operate

---

[9]E. Potthoff, O. Blume, and H. Duvernell, *Zwischenbilanz der
Mitbestimmung* (Tubingen: J.C.B. Mohr, 1962), p. 145. About half
the labor directors indicated that they had additional training
after leaving school.

[10]Defined as having two of the following three characteristics:
more than 20,000 employees, a turnover of at least $250 million
a year, or a total capital of $125 million.

against the wishes of the personnel of the company. All directors are thus to be appointed by the executive committee of the supervisory board, which is to consist of an equal number of shareholder and labor representatives. This has been questioned by the unions because the full supervisory board with its stockholder majority could overturn decisions of its executive committee.

The proposal of the government—a compromise between the divergent views of the two government coalition parties, the Social Democrats and the Free Democrats—aims mainly at strengthening the position of the Works Council, especially in questions of dismissals. A major issue was the demand of the trade unions for free access of their representatives to workshops and offices, and authority for them to recruit members on the premises. A dispute also arose as to the right of executive staff members to be represented by the unions. Prolonged efforts were necessary to obtain a compromise acceptable to the two parties represented in the government: the Social Democrats, eager to satisfy the union demands, and the Democrats, who are closer to management. The outcome is summarized below on page 95.

Labor-management relations were remarkably peaceful until the strike wave of 1969. This was partly the result of labor legislation, which requires that conciliation procedures must be exhausted before a strike can be lawfully called and that 75 percent of the union members must approve a strike in a secret ballot. Strike benefits are paid only if the governing body of the union approves the strike. On the employers' side, considerable social and business pressure is exerted to induce companies to join the employers' association of their industry. Once they are members they are no longer legally free to conclude an agreement with the union. Lockouts are permitted and have indeed been used on occasion, with considerable effect. More important than legislation in maintaining peaceful labor relations has been the remarkable long-term economic boom in West Germany after the devastation wrought by World War II and its consequences. In the early postwar years the unions exerted a good deal of self-restraint, partly because they understood the economic requirements of rapid reconstruction, partly because of the fear of runaway inflation, and partly because they only slowly regained their self-confidence after their destruction by the Nazis.

The rapid economic expansion has also permitted the West German economy to absorb several million German-speaking immigrants driven out of their former settlements in other areas of Europe, especially the Sudetenland in Czechoslovakia, Transylvania, and so on. Indeed, given the labor shortage that soon developed in many countries of the European continent, these immigrants proved a boon to the German economy. So urgent was the desire for additional manpower that German industry re-

cruited labor in Italy, Spain, Yugoslavia, Turkey, and other
countries by the hundreds of thousands—as did Switzerland,
France, Sweden, Austria, and other industrial nations. Although this influx has lessened inflationary pressures on the
labor market by greatly increasing the supply of labor, it has
tended to favor profits relative to wages—a factor that contributed to the explosive tensions of 1969 and the subsequent
union drives for wage increases vastly in excess of productivity increases.

The German-speaking immigrants from Eastern Europe were
received as full citizens in West Germany and were openly welcomed by the unions, but the so-called guest workers from non-
German-speaking areas were treated as temporary visitors. They
may of course enter the unions and participate in elections of
workers' councils, and under new legislation enacted in 1971
may be elected to the councils.[11]

For many of them the host country provides the first experience of trade unionism. In order to do this effectively the
unions have organized German language courses for foreign workers, and some unions publish material in foreign languages.
One union (the German mineworkers') has appointed an education
officer with a Turkish trade union background, who has been
made a member of the union's executive board. Various agreements have been concluded for an exchange of information between German unions and those of other countries such as Italy,
Yugoslavia, and Turkey. In general the attempts to integrate
foreign workers into the unions of their host country appear to
succeed best with younger workers. The unions of the European
Economic Community have recently asked that foreign workers be
given the same legal status and social benefits that nationals
of the six countries now enjoy.

The DGB plays no significant part in the bargaining activities of the affiliated unions, although it is empowered to
issue guidelines to them.[12] Instead it has devoted a good
deal of its energy to political issues. Thus it opposed German

---

[11]In Switzerland, where the proportion of "guest workers" to
native population came close to 20 percent, measures were taken
to reduce the number of guest workers; in particular, they are
only rarely permitted to bring their families, a fact which in
itself tends to limit the number of foreign workers seeking admission to the country.

[12]An interesting result of this fact, but also a symptom of the
relatively limited significance of bargaining in the totality
of union activities, is the absence of any reference to collective bargaining in the fairly elaborate—twenty printed pages—
"Basic Program of the DGB," adopted in 1963.

rearmament, the equipment of the armed forces with atomic weapons, the so-called Emergency Laws of 1968, and so on. In most of these campaigns the DGB found itself to the left of the SPD, closer to the traditions of the German labor movement than the political party now aimed toward becoming a "people's party." The contrast is particularly sharp in the case of the largest industrial union affiliated with the DGB, the I. G. Metall (metalworkers' union). Its 2 million members represent almost one-third of the total DGB membership, and its leader Otto Brenner, the most powerful single figure in the labor movement, although in no ways pro-Communist is clearly associated with the left of center currents in the SPD. There is no indication, however, that this tension will lead to a real conflict between the party and the unions in the near future.

7

The French Pattern

French collective bargaining appears especially strange
to the American and perhaps even to the British observer in
both its origins and its present state. The slow progress of
industrialization until 1945—in sharp contrast to the rapid
economic expansion of the fifties and sixties—as well as Syndicalist and revolutionary Marxian ideas and the violent political events of French history during the last eighty years have
delayed the advance of collective bargaining compared with that
of most other industrial nations.

Government and legislation play a more important role in
industrial relations in France than in many other Western countries. First, law and administrative action determine many
fringe benefits, although collective agreements have provided
either for supplements to the legal arrangements—as in the
case of old age pensions (1957)—or added social benefits
(agreements on employment and vocational education, 1969-70)
more frequently since the late fifties. Second, collective
bargaining itself takes place at rather high levels—sometimes
covering the entire nation, sometimes covering a region. Government representatives take part in the meetings.[1] A further
remarkable feature of the system is the fact that many supplementary social benefits were the result of agreements concluded
by the union confederations—that is, above the industry level
(comparable with agreements concluded by the AFL-CIO). Unilateral determination of wages and working conditions is still
fairly widespread because unions are relatively weak, but undoubtedly they exert some indirect influence, party by the "extension" of agreements by administrative action and partly by
the "sympathetic" influence of the terms of collective agree-

---

[1]The impact of planning on industrial relations has been discussed in chapter 4.

ments. Since the fifties, however, collective bargaining has
gained greatly in importance.

Apart from a short period following World War I, collective bargaining on a significant scale started in 1936 under
the pressure of sit-down strikes and the coming into power of
the Popular Front government of Léon Blum. In the long process
leading to this event the government had to overcome not only
the resistance of the French employers, who preferred to maintain the old "master-in-our-own house" attitude, but also the
weakness and ideological divisions of the French labor organizations, some of which rejected collective bargaining as a be-
trayal of the class struggle.

As late as 1919—after the downfall of revolutionary syndicalism during World War I—the main trade union federation,
Confédération Générale du Travail (CGT), finally came out in
favor of collective agreements and concluded a small number
under a new law, enacted on March 25, 1919. The organization
of the Communist-led CGTU (Confédération Générale du Travail
Unitaire), which split from the CGT, and the general decline
of the labor organizations soon ended this first major attempt
at establishing a system of collective agreements.

The historic Matignon agreement of June 7, 1936, made a
new beginning.[2] Following the agreement a law enacted in June
1936 made a deliberate effort to adjust the system of collective agreements to the conditions of a country in which trade
unions were weak in membership, unstable, and divided by phil-
osophical, religious, and other considerations. The law therefore provided that collective agreements were to be concluded
by "joint commissions" combining spokesmen of the "most representative organizations" of employers and employees in the
presence of government representatives. The minister of labor
was given power to extend these collective agreements, in full
or in part, to all enterprises of the same industry within the
territory specified in the agreement. In this way the private
contract acquired the power of a public decree, and the observ-
ance of its wage clauses could be enforced by the methods applicable to any other public decree. In addition to private
action, such "extended" agreements therefore had the power of
penal sanction as far as wages were concerned. The joint commission appeared as a quasi-public organ which made laws when
the minister of labor approved. The fact that the minister
could not change the agreement but at the most could restrict
its extension to certain provisions, confirmed the "legislative

---

[2]An excellent survey is provided in Jean-Daniel Reynaud, *Les
Syndicats en France*, 2d ed. (Paris: Armand Colin, 1966), and in
Val R. Lorwin, *The French Labor Movement* (Cambridge: Harvard
University Press, 1964).

power" of the commission, as did the fact that the extended
agreement lost its validity when the original agreement expired
or was changed. [3]

As a result of this system there were two types of collective agreements in France: those that were valid only for the
parties to the contract, and those that were endowed with general validity. Some 5,880 agreements of the first kind and
some 680 of the second kind were concluded between 1936 and
1939. [4] As these figures indicate, the enactment of the law of
1936 was followed by the conclusion of a large number of agreements. Trade union membership rose to staggering heights; the
merger of the CGT and the CGTU in March 1936 enhanced the power
and prestige of trade unionism. This halcyon period lasted
only a few years, however, because the two partners split again
in 1939 over the issue of the Nazi-Soviet pact concluded that
year.

One of the main consequences of the law of 1936 was that
it became necessary to define the concept *most representative
organizations*, particularly on the trade union side. For even
after the temporary merger of CGT and CGTU in 1936, French
trade unionism remained split into a number of rival organizations in addition to the CGT—the Christian unions of the CFTC
(Confédération Française des Travailleurs Chrétiens), a fore-
men's and engineer's union, the CGC, [5] and a large number of unaffiliated, so-called autonomous unions were the most important. A 1936 circular from the minister of labor to his staff
indicated that more than one organization might be described as
"most representative." This contradicted the interpretation
given by Prime Minister Léon Blum during the parliamentary debates preceding the adoption of the law, but the practice has
followed the circular rather than Blum's statement.

Thus interpreted, the concept *most representative organization* has survived to this day. It was retained in the emergency legislation enacted at the outbreak of World War II, when

---

[3]It is interesting to compare this method with the American
method of "extension" introduced by the establishment of "exclusive bargaining rights" combined with the majority principle
of the Wagner Act.

[4]Jean Brèthe de la Bressaye, "Le Nouveau Statut des Conventions
Collectives de Travail," *Droit Social* 10, no. 3 (March 1947).

[5]Confédération Générale des Cadres de l'Economie Française,
created in 1937. Since 1944 this organization has dropped the
last three words in its name and reduced the conventional ab-
breviation to CGC. It organizes salaried and technical employees.

the "most representative" labor organizations were empowered
to designate the candidates for election as "délégués du personnel," a kind of shop steward. After the war the sample
principle was used to establish the lists of candidates for the
election of the comités d'entreprise (joint committees of labor and management formed to deal with any question affecting
the welfare of the workers and to consult on issues relating to
the general functioning of the enterprise). Struggles arose
between organizations over admittance to the circle of "most
representative" organizations. In the end, the three main organizations then existing for all categories of employees were
admitted: CGT, CGT-FO, and CFTC;[6] and for the discussion of
collective agreements relating to the higher staff, the CGC
was admitted. For agreements referring only to particular
groups or of limited though national significance, the minister
of labor may designate other organizations as "most representative."

The development of collective agreements, which had been
given a powerful impetus by the law of 1936, and the rapid
growth of the trade unions did not last long. The failure of
the general strike on November 30, 1938, and the renewal of the
conflict between Communists and non-Communists in the CGT were
accompanied by a rapid loss of members. The outbreak of World
War II completed the reversal of the trend toward bargaining.
A decree of October 27, 1939, stabilized working conditions
"for the duration" at the level of September 1. Other decrees,
of November 10, 1939, and June 1, 1940, gave the minister of
labor the authority to fix wages. The Vichy regime set up after the defeat of France by Nazi Germany dissolved the trade
union confederations and employers' federations by the "law" of
August 16, 1940. The revival of collective bargaining had to
wait for the liberation of the country, although for a long period after 1945 the minister of labor continued to determine
wages, and uniform wage changes were decreed several times by
government authority.

On December 23, 1946, a unanimous decision of Parliament,
adopted almost without discussion, marked what was intended to
be a first stop toward a return to collective bargaining. In
essence the new law enabled the joint commissions to meet again

---

[6]The latter changed its name in 1964 to French Democratic Confederation of Labor (Confédération Française Démocratique du
Travail, CFDT). A minority group kept the old title and split
from the CFDT. It was promptly designated "most representative." There are thus now four "most representative" confederations. CGT-FO (FO: Force Ouvrière) is a non-Communist federation that broke with the CGT after World War II for ideological
reasons.

and to determine working conditions; wages continued to remain
within the province of the minister. This, it was claimed, was
necessary because of the inflationary effects of ill-considered
wage increases. Only one agreement was concluded under this
law, mainly because of the exclusion of wages from bargaining.

The pressure for unrestricted collective bargaining increased sharply, the more so as price controls and rationing
were rapidly abandoned. In 1950 the government gave in and
maintained its position on only two major points: (1) The Minister of Labor remains free to decide in the light of circumstances whether to extend collective agreements to workers and
employers not represented by the partners to the agreement.
(2) The determination of a national minimum wage for all occupations—called *minimum vital* (then SMIG and now SMIC in French
labor parlance)—is to be carried out by the government-appointed Higher Commission of Collective Agreements on the basis
of a family budget, but the government itself makes the final
decision. Minimum wages for different occupations can of
course be set higher than the minimum vital in the collective
agreements.[7]

In its essentials the law enacted in February 1950 returned to the principles of 1919 and 1936. The role of the
government was thus restricted principally to calling meetings
of the joint commissions, to deciding whether to extend the
agreement or not or only certain parts of it, and to determining the minimum wage. In some respects the new law showed
originality, as, for example, in the requirement that collective agreements contain a clause providing for equal pay for
equal work for men and women; it also provided that the labor
inspectors have the right to control the application of all
parts of an extended agreement, not only of the wage clauses,
as in the past.

---

[7]This form of the guaranteed minimum wage was replaced in 1952
by a system providing for almost immediate adjustment to cost-
of-living changes. In 1967 a linkage to economic growth was
added. The minimum wage is thus to be adjusted according to
either of two principles: changes in the cost-of-living index
or in line with general economic conditions, especially the
evolution of the national product. The latter clause was introduced officially in 1967, but even prior to this large increases in the minimum wage beyond the rise of the index occurred, beginning in 1954. A very substantial increase in 1968
brought the minimum wage closer to the general wage rise since
1950. See Jules Milhau, "Indexation des salaires sur le coût
de la vie," *Droit Social* 32 (September-October 1969). This
evolution has put even greater stress on the government's role
in setting the minimum wage.

Yet by this time the ability of French trade unions to engage in effective bargaining had greatly weakened compared to
the immediate postwar situation. French trade unionism is divided into many competitive organizations. At the time of the
Accords Matignon in 1936, the intention was probably to make
eligible for collective bargaining the "most representative"
union only, after the principle of exclusive bargaining rights
under the American Wagner Act. This, as was pointed out above,
soon proved politically impossible, because the CGT would have
had a monopoly in almost all branches of industrial activity,
whereas the Christian unions would have been restricted to a
few sections of trade and commerce. To this Parliament objected violently. Thus, the principle of multiunion representation in collective bargaining was accepted, but it led inevitably to two consequences: greatly increased difficulties in
arriving at agreements and a prolonged struggle for a change
in the method of selection of the "most representative" union.
Union rivalry at the conference table expressed itself in competitive demands. Every union endeavored to demonstrate that
its competitor was "giving in" too readily to the employers,
and the union representatives were reluctant to accept reasonable compromises out of fear of their rivals. To demonstrate
that no better result could be obtained, the unions tolerated
strikes with or without official approval—sometimes with the
result that even the previously obtained concessions were lost.
     The struggle for admission to the charmed circle of "most
representative unions" was essentially waged with political
weapons, since in the last resort the minister decided. Thus
French labor relations were (and continue to be) dependent to
a large extent on the political influence of each union; to
another part they were determined by the undeniable fact that
in many enterprises a contract without the (at least tacit)
approval of the CGT union was likely to be ineffective.
     The fact that the largest of the trade union centers, the
CGT, is dominated by the Communist party is one of the most important features of the industrial relations scene. Labor relations are often a function not only of the issues arising
between French workers and their employers but also of the relations between the French Communist party and the French government, or even between the Soviet and the French governments.
Thus the first postwar years, when the Communists were represented in the government and Franco-Russian relations were
fairly harmonious, were extraordinarily quiet in the factories
as well. After the summer of 1947, when the Communists had
left the government and the Marshall Plan was beginning to em-
bitter Franco-Russian relations, successive waves of strikes
expressed at the same time the social dissatisfaction of the
workers, the political struggle in France, and the changing dip-
lomatic relations between the Soviet Union and France. Collec-

tive bargaining requires that both parties be prepared to accept common-sense compromises and ultimate cooperation, and it
is difficult to see how bargaining can successfully operate as
long as foreign policy dominates the scene. However, since
about the middle of the fifties this factor has had a diminish-
ing influence on industrial relations; the CGT has been forced
to recognize that it is becoming difficult to mobilize the
workers for purely political ends.

For a long time the non-Communist unions refused to cooperate with the CGT unions, although individual unions occasionally departed from this policy. The systematic effort at iso-
lating the CGT—by far the largest of the labor confederations
—rarely fully successful, broke down partly as a result of a
split within the Christian trade union federation (CFTC). As
was mentioned earlier, the majority of the latter had dropped
the term *Christian* from its name in 1964 and had renamed itself
the French Democratic Confederation of Labor (Confédération
Française Démocratique du Travail, CFDT), although a minority
retained the old name. In January 1966 the CFDT and the CGT
entered into a joint-action agreement for a limited number of
purposes, among them the right of the unions to operate in the
plant. This objective appeared to have been attained when the
agreement of May 27, 1968[8] (following the great strikes of that
month), contained a promise that a law would be introduced to
authorize the operation of the unions in the plant. Yet the
same strike movement also marked the beginning of the end of
the cooperation between the two federations. The CGT, in a
significant revelation of its actual role in the movements of
that year, accused the CFDT of being too friendly toward left-
ists in general and left-wing student groups in particular. At
the same time, the CFDT moved toward cooperation with the Force
Ouvrière (FO). Because the CFDT has officially disavowed its
religious commitment, it is difficult to see why cooperation
should not result in a merger. This, however, might require
personal sacrifices from the leaders of both groups, and there
is little evidence so far of a readiness to accept such sacrifices.

The CGT and the CFDT cooperated again in the strike movements in the fall of 1969 and early 1970. Even the FO, which
usually kept apart from common action with the CGT, was drawn
into a unified resistance movement against the "Loi Anticas-
seur," a legislative proposal which would render the organizers
of demonstrations liable for damages occurring in connection
with the demonstrations. Thus the issue of united union activity remains on the agenda.

---

[8]See footnote 11.

Difficulties for an effective bargaining system are not only or even primarily on the workers' side. Most French employers have accepted collective bargaining only as a lesser evil than government determination of wages. The unions have little reason to believe that the majority of employers have really abandoned their "master-in-my-own house" ideas. Neither employers nor workers have any sustained experience in collective bargaining.

Employers' hostility toward unionism found its clearest expression in the employers' refusal to tolerate union presence in the plant. One of the roots of this traditional attitude is the prevalence of small and medium-sized plants in the country. Labor relations in these plants are usually handled in a personal way, and the intervention of the union is regarded as intolerable and unnecessary outside interference that is contrary to the highly developed sense of secrecy in French business. Even after the high rate of economic expansion in the fifties and sixties, small enterprises still employ more than half the gainfully occupied population, but the evolution has been clearly in favor of modern, large-scale enterprises, which by now employ about one-third of the country's labor force.

The division of the unions also contributed to the separation between the unions and the plant. In 1936 the CGT, conscious of different unions and large numbers of unorganized workers in the plants, proposed that the délégués du personnel (shop stewards) be elected by all workers, and the legislation then enacted and reaffirmed after World War II so provided.[9] In the same way, the plant committees (or workers' councils—comités d'entreprise), created in 1945 and 1946 as organs of industrial democracy, are elected by all employees; the unions merely have the right to propose lists of candidates for the first round of the election, in which a clear majority is required; if there is no majority a second election is held, in which other candidates can be nominated. Unions may also be represented without vote at the committee meetings. Apart from this, the union was visible in the plant only by way of its posted announcements, and even this modest right was interpreted in a highly restrictive way by the courts.

The contrast between this traditional mode of thinking in labor relations and the rapidly changing and modernizing eco-

---

[9] Later union publications, however, leave no doubt that the unions realized the need for union representatives operating in the plant. One example is the unsuccessful joint union proposal of a model collective agreement in the metal industry in 1949, quoted in François Sellier, *Stratégie de la lutte sociale, France, 1936-1960* (Paris: Economie et Humanisme [Les Editions Ouvriéres], 1961).

nomic structure of the country was reflected in a number of
symptoms of tension. The most spectacular was the great crisis
of May 1968. Until then the Fifth Republic had made only modest contributions to the adjustment of labor relations to the
changing economic structure.[10] One of the major reforms following the upheaval concerned the status of the union in the
enterprise.[11] One part of the Accords de Grenelle—the agreement settling the strikes of May 1968—provided for legislation
on the subject.

Briefly, the law compels the employer to recognize the existence and operation of branches of representative unions upon
their demand in all enterprises employing fifty persons or more
and of union delegates designated by the union leadership[12] and
employed by the enterprise for more than a year. The delegates
are protected against dismissal in the same way as the elected
representatives of the personnel (personnel delegates, members
of the plant committees)—that is, they can be dismissed only
with the approval of the (government) labor inspector. Violation of this clause may call for compensation for the unjustly
discharged union delegate and for fines or imprisonment of the
plant manager, but in spite of union pressure, not for the re-
instatement of the union delegate.[13] A certain number of paid
working hours is made available to the delegates for their
work, but only in enterprises with at least 150 employees. The
functions and rights of union branches and delegates in the
plant are not spelled out in detail in the law. In general, it

---

[10]Legislation banishing discrimination in employment because of
union activities was enacted in April 1956, before de Gaulle
came to power. A law on plant committees passed in 1966 somewhat strengthened the role of the unions in the plant.

[11]J. Brèthe de la Bressaye, "La présence du syndicat dans l'enterprise," *Droit Social* 32, no. 3 (March 1969). The background
is well presented in Sellier, *Stratégie de la lutte sociale*,
especially part 3. A few agreements, especially on the plant
level, concluded between 1961 and 1965 did admit that either
union locals or union delegates operate in the plant.

[12]This solution rather than election by the branch membership
has been the result of a lengthy tug-of-war between the minister and the national Assembly. Another issue—between the
larger confederations (CGT, CFDT) and Parliament—concerned the
number of delegates. The unions wanted this to depend on union
support at the elections of the plant committee; the law makes
the number proportionate to employment.

[13]In this the law follows French tradition.

would seem that they coincide with those of similar institutions elsewhere, although only experience will tell for certain.[14] Whether the handling of grievances is to be left to
the personnel delegate or to be passed on to the union representatives is equally unsettled, and this lack of clarity could
become a source of serious conflicts between the union and non-
unionized personnel.

Although the applicability of the law is limited to enterprises of at least fifty employees, so that only two-thirds of
the employees in industry and one-quarter of those in trade are
covered, the law, if effective in these sectors, could mark the
beginning of a new era for French unionism. To the extent to
which the union enters the daily life and concerns of the worker, it could substitute its down-to-earth action for the declining appeal of traditional ideologies. Whether the existing
structure and the resources of French unionism will permit it
to make this radical readjustment in the foreseeable future is
doubtful. Yet no less a person than the secretary general of
the CGT has described the new law as "certainly the most important legal victory of the trade union movement since the law of
1884," which provided the legal basis for trade unionism.[15]

Since December 1963 the National Employment Fund has gradually extended its scope of activity.[16] In the case of mass
layoffs, the labor inspectors retain not only the legal power
to approve or reject, which had been given to them by decree in
May 1945, but also financial means of intervention. They can
use funds to support geographic and occupational relocation of
the workers concerned, provide enterprises with the means to
permit early retirement, arrange for retraining, compensate
workers who were compelled to accept lower-paying jobs, and so
on.

As a result of the Protocol of Grenelle, a national agreement on job security was reached between the various union confederations and the two major employer federations. It gives

---

[14]The relationship between union, union delegates, union
branch, shop stewards, and works' committee members is also
left to be worked out in the future.

[15]Quoted in Guy Caire's column, "La situation sociale," *Droit
Social* 32, no. 3 (March 1969): 181.

[16]It is significant that this institution, like so many others
in the industrial relations field in France, goes back to an
"interprofessional agreement"—that is, an agreement of the
confederations, this one concluded in 1958. Decision-making
occurs more and more frequently at levels far removed from the
workers in the plant and even from the individual union.

the workers' councils a say in collective dismissals on economic grounds.   The unions—on a national or regional level—are
represented on vocational committees, which are essentially instruments of mutual information between labor and management.
Surprisingly, the unions have failed to assume a direct role in
mass dismissals in the individual plants—a failure in sharp
contrast with their desire to play a larger part in industrial
relations in the plant.[17]

------

[17]*International Labour Review* 100, no. 3 (September 1969): 273-
74; Jacques Villebrun, "La loi du 18 decembre 1963," *Droit Social* 28, no. 2 (February 1965), and *Droit Social* 32, no. 4
(April 1969).

8

Workers' Councils

Whatever the nature of collective agreements, as John T. Dunlop has pointed out, the work place is organized, in a formal or an informal way. There are matters such as piece rates and many details of working conditions that can only be settled at the work place, and if the collective agreement covers a multitude of plants, formal or informal supplements fitted to the special conditions of each plant are required, unless their determination is left to the unilateral decision of the employer. Bargaining at the shop level—the conclusion of supplementary and detailed agreements, the settlement of individual grievances—may be carried on by union representatives or by persons who represent the entire work force, whether unionized or not. The first solution is frequently adopted in Britain; the second is typical for the Continent, especially Germany and France. The terminology also varies: the British speak of shop stewards, the Germans of works' council members, the French of members of the enterprise committee and personnel delegates.[1] A British definition would describe the shop stewards as "trade union lay representatives at the place of work."[2] The institution which is roughly the shop steward's counterpart in Germany and France is officially—and quite often also in fact—representative of all the workers, whether they are union members or not, and is thus not an agent of the union.

---

[1] For simplicity's sake we shall use the terms *council member* and *shop steward* as equivalent, even though their status and role may be quite different, depending on the country concerned.

[2] W.E.J. McCarthy, "The Role of Shop Stewards in British Industrial Relations," Research Paper No. 1 of the Royal Commission on Trade Unions and Employers' Associations (London: H.M. Stationery Office, 1967), p. 4.

ORIGINS

The functions of shop stewards have grown considerably over the last quarter of a century, although there were occasions in earlier periods—such as during World War I and immediately after in Britain—when they played a highly significant role. In Britain the shop stewards' movement of World War I was associated with Guild socialism, a form of workers' self-government in the plant. Another root of the councils, predominantly on the Continent, is the workers' and soldiers' councils established during the Russian Revolution in 1917 (and before, during the abortive revolutionary attempt of 1905). This origin, although it gives the councils tremendous appeal among left-wing workers, has often confused the issue of what the councils are really about. A third source of the institution, of significance in Germany and Austria-Hungary, is the emergency created by World War I. In order to ensure peaceful industrial relations and orderly production in the factories while hostilities lasted, the imperial governments of the two leading Central Powers proposed a "deal" to the labor organizations: the government offered the unions protection for elected members of workers' committees against dismissal and discrimination in exchange for union cooperation in the war effort— essentially a no-strike pledge. This agreement was embodied in the German Auxiliary Service Law of 1916.[3] Because until then the unions had encountered almost insuperable difficulties in protecting their members and especially their leaders against employers' discrimination in the plants, most union leaders regarded the proposed legislation "as a great step forward in the process of union recognition by the employers."[4] There were some warnings that since the committee members were to be elected by all workers, whether union members or not, they would be independent of the unions and would thus diminish the latter's authority, but most union leaders welcomed the legislation.

When the employers' association recognized the union federation as the legitimate representative of the workers at the time of the revolution of 1918, the agreement referred to matters "above the plant level" (*überbetrieblich*) rather than to the work place itself. Thus the wartime workers' committees continued to exist, on the basis of a government decree, and then were replaced by workers' councils elected under a law enacted in 1920. The status of the workers' councils was at

---

[3]See Sturmthal, *Workers Councils: A Study of Workplace Organization on Both Sides of the Iron Curtain* (Cambridge: Harvard University Press, 1964).

[4]Ibid., p. 13.

first ambiguous. Some saw in the councils simply a barely con-
cealed way by which the unions could extend their influence into the plants. Revolutionaries, eager to transplant the councils, Russian style, into the nascent Weimar Republic, hoped
that the councils would "supersede what they regarded as the
bureaucratic and official-ridden organization of the Trade Unions by a new type of organization based solely on the Councils
System and imbued with the revolutionary spirit in contrast to
the timid reformist socialism of which the government and the
Trade Union leaders were adherents."[5] Others saw in the councils the beginnings of the management of Socialist industry,
and still another group viewed them as the cornerstones of the
public administration of a future Socialist Germany. From the
beginning, therefore, the issue of the relationship between the
councils and the unions arose. When the legislation of 1920
was framed some of the unions were greatly concerned about this
relationship. The law of 1920 appeared to subordinate the
councils to the trade unions, even though the councils were assigned distinct, but complementary, functions, and it thus
eliminated the plans of those who wished to turn the councils
into revolutionary or managerial bodies—a decision which was
confirmed by a national congress of workers' councils held the
same year.

Still, the failure of the unions to enter the plants themselves, the fact that the councils were elected by members of
different and competitive unions as well as by nonunionists and
were thus often internally divided, and the absence of effective sanctions the councils could use against recalcitrant employers all led to considerable tension between councils and
unions and to a congenital weakness of union structure. One of
the roots—perhaps the most important one—of what we have
called the administrative union is in the council system.

The French plant committees or workers' councils—comités
d'entreprise—arose as late as the end of World War II. The
Popular Front government of 1936—based on Socialists, Radicals, and Communists—sponsored an agreement between union and
employers' confederations which, among other things, provided
for the election of personnel delegates (délégués du personnel)
to handle grievances. The plant committees, which resemble the
German workers' councils in many respects, came into being under the de Gaulle regime, which followed the liberation of the
country in 1945.

A similar institution are the plant committees (commissione interne) established in Italy. They originated in col-

---

[5]C. W. Guillebaud, *The Works Council: A German Experiment in
Industrial Democracy* (Cambridge: Harvard University Press,
1928), pp. 8-9.

lective agreements as far back as 1919 and served as grievance
committees and handled internal plant problems.[6]   Although
these early committees were elected by union members alone, the
recreated commissions after World War II were to be elected by
all workers, according to proportional representation. This
change came under bitter attack at a later stage, partly because the "Internal Commission," it was said, "is the alibi of
the non-unionized workers, who believe they are being shrewd
and believe they have fulfilled a duty of conscience through
the expression of an annual suffrage. How can one think of being able to create trade union strength with a renunciation of
such a kind, which becomes a principal element for the de-
unionization of the workers?"[7]   Austria essentially followed
the German example in the structure and functions of the councils, but the authority of the trade unions was at all times so
great that little if any friction developed between councils
and unions. Enterprise unions similar in some respects to the
enterprise unions of Japan evolved in a number of developing
countries in Latin America, Asia, and Africa. In these cases
the union representatives at the plant level are in fact the
president and the other members of the executive committee of
the union.[8]

THE BRITISH SHOP STEWARD

"Most unions since the war," says Anthony Sampson,[9] referring to the situation after World War II, "have been challenged
by 'wildcat strikes' and rebellious shop-stewards. It is the
shop stewards who collect union dues at the factories, recruit
new members, and enforce the factory agreements: the T[rans-
port] and G[eneral] Workers' Union has 25,000 of them, and altogether there are said to be 200,000—more shop stewards than
soldiers." Other authors are more cautious in their estimates,

---

[6]Daniel L. Horowitz, *The Italian Labor Movement* (Cambridge:
Harvard University Press, 1963), pp. 143-44.

[7]*Sindacato Nuovo* (a publication of CISL, a non-Communist, principally Christian trade union confederation), July 1959, as
quoted in Horowitz, *Italian Labor Movement,* p. 315.

[8]International Labour Office, "Rights of Trade Union Representatives at the Level of the Undertaking," Labor-Management Relations Series, No. 32, ILO, Geneva, 1969, p. 8 and passim.

[9]*Anatomy of Britain Today* (New York: Harper & Row, Publishers,
1965), p. 606.

but they agree that 200,000 may not be far off the facts, especially since the number of shop stewards is increasing more rapidly than union membership.

The rules under which they operate are diverse but not very important. In fact, the shop stewards often perform functions and exert power substantially at variance with the rules. In any case, there is little doubt that they play an increasingly important role in determining effective wages and working conditions, in many cases independently from and often against the will of the trade union leadership. They have even engaged in collective bargaining at the plant level and have used strikes and other devices to obtain better terms than those of the national agreements, although these plant-level understandings have often been informal. Indeed, the Donovan Commission referred to the operations of the shop stewards as the basic element in a second industrial relations system that is often far more important than the system of the official collective agreements.

The relations between the stewards and the unions are intricate. Officially the stewards—elected by union members and engaged in collecting union dues—represent the union in the plant. Quite often they are the only union representative the great majority of rank-and-file members ever see. However, most unions find it extremely difficult, often impossible, to maintain control of or even contact with the stewards. British unions, as a rule, are poor because membership dues are low. As a consequence they have few officials and, in the case of a strike, have little material assistance to offer or to withhold from a union group. Moreover, the nature of multifirm agreements makes supplementary understandings at the plant level inevitable. Piece rates, job evaluation, special allowances, and working conditions can hardly be determined in detail in multiplant agreements covering large areas, as most British agreements do. Moreover, in times of labor shortage management may take the initiative in approaching the stewards to negotiate ways of attracting or holding labor and of improving productivity.[10] As a result, shop stewards call strikes and engage in other forms of pressure—with or without the approval of the union. The "unofficial" strike about which so much has been said and written in Britain is only one of the many ways in which shop stewards—on their own or sometimes with the silent, more or less reluctantly given, approval of the union—aim to attain their objectives.[11] There are, of course, many cases in

---

[10]The so-called productivity agreements in British industry are one example of such bargaining.

[11]See the extended discussion of the varied means of pressure at the disposal of the shop stewards in McCarthy, "Shop Stew-

which management prefers to deal with shop stewards rather than
with the union, because the informal agreements with the stewards are more readily changed and concessions made in them are
often more easily withdrawn than those in formal written agreements with the union. Moreover, managers are frequently reluctant for their concessions to shop stewards to be publicized,
and informal, unwritten agreements are more readily kept secret.[12]

Yet the stewards are indispensable for the life of the union, because attendance at union meetings is notoriously low,
and the collection of union dues depends on the stewards. However, the weakness of most British unions in funds and manpower
has prevented them from training stewards adequately and from
maintaining close contact with them, which has produced the division of the British industrial relations system into two
parts, to which the Donovan Commission referred.

THE GERMAN WORKS' COUNCIL

The importance and vitality of the workers' councils in
Germany was demonstrated at the end of World War II. As soon
as the Nazi system was destroyed in a town, the workers elected workers' councils to represent them. The Western occupation authorities gave only reluctant approval to the institution and limited the councils essentially to advisory activities. The workers, arguing that big business had supported
the Nazi regime and that therefore the councils would be able
to prevent a recurrence of antidemocratic actions of the large
enterprises, asked that the councils be given the right to
participate in managerial decision-making. In two states of
the Western zones of occupation, Hesse and Württemberg-Baden,

---

[11](cont'd.) ards in British Industrial Relations." Particularly interesting is his discussion of what he calls the "endemic
strike situation" in one engineering establishment.

[12]A by-product of the growth of shop-floor handling of industrial relations has been the decline and often disappearance
of joint consultative committees, which during and after World
War II were hailed as cornerstones of a developing system of
industrial democracy. On the whole, the consultative committees seem to have survived and to have played a significant
role only "where unionization and shop-steward representation
is nonexistent or weak" (Ibid., p. 34).

laws to this effect were enacted. However, the U.S. military
authorities suspended these sections of the law, claiming that
such fundamental issues should be settled at the federal level
—an argument union circles did not universally take at its
face value.

The Works Constitution Law, enacted in October 1952, which
covers all enterprises, private and public—the latter if they
are organized as share or limited-liability companies—provided
the legal foundation for the councils.[13] A year before legislation specifically applying to coal and steel—the Codetermination Law—had been enacted. Reference to this was made in
chapter 6; here it is sufficient to remind the reader that for
these two industries labor representation was provided in two
of their three governing bodies, the board of supervision and
the management board, but not in the assembly of the stockholders. On the board—frequently consisting of eleven members—
five members represent labor, five the stockholders, and the
eleventh man is selected jointly. Of the five labor members,
two represent the workers' council—one the blue-collar workers, the other the white-collar workers—two are designated by
the DGB in agreement with the unions represented in the plant,
and the fifth labor member, also designated by the union confederation, is independent of the enterprise. Labor representation on the managing board—usually a three-man group—consists of a labor director who must have the approval of the
majority of the labor members on the supervisory board, which
makes the selection.[14] The role of the labor director has
aroused doubt and criticism abroad. His loyalty is divided between the workers, to whom he owes his position, and the enterprise, which he now serves. To avoid such conflicts of loyalty
the British unions decided that board members of the nationalized enterprises could no longer be union representatives and
had to "surrender any responsibility to the Trade Union" upon
their appointment to the board. Still, until the strains of
1969 and the wildcat strikes very few symptoms indicated tensions arising from possible conflicts of loyalty. In general,
workers employed in codetermination establishments reportedly
think that the system has brought them a number of advan-

---

[13]In a modified form it applies also to the *Tendenzbetriebe*,
establishments primarily serving political, trade union, char-
itable, educational, scientific, or artistic purposes.

[14]For further details, background, and so on see Sturmthal,
Workers' Councils. For boards with more than eleven members,
proportionate adjustments in labor and stockholders' representation is foreseen.

tages.[15]   Outside of this group positive views of codetermination are harder to find.   Only one of every five Germans and one of every three employees holds a favorable view of the institution.   Nor does there seem to be a widespread urge to expand the system to other industries, even though the unions have made this one of their main objectives.

At the time of its enactment, the law represented an acceptable compromise for the two ideological currents that merged in the new confederation (DGB).   For the Social Democrats (SPD) it was a possible substitute for the nationalization of industry, which neither the American occupation force nor the domestic political evolution of West Germany permitted. Moreover, nationalization of industry had come to be identified with communism because it was so radically applied in the Soviet-occupied parts of Germany.   The Christian (CDU) wing of the unions, guided by Catholic theoreticians, found codetermination, a system of cooperation between capital and labor, very much to its liking.   Thus the new demand offered an excellent ideological foundation for the merger of the two currents in the post-World War II labor movement.

The Works Constitution Law applies to both codetermination industries and other industrial enterprises.   It sets up in enterprises a council of at least five employees; the size of the council is in rough proportion to that of the labor force.   As a rule there are separate elections for manual workers and white-collar workers; all employees about eighteen years of age may vote; employees above twenty-one may be elected.   Since 1968, according to a Common Market decision, foreign workers from the six countries are eligible to serve as council members.   A new works' constitution law enacted late in 1971 extended this right to all foreign workers.   Union representatives may be invited to participate in the council meetings without voting privileges.

Because the councils are designed to cooperate with management, they may not call strikes or use other methods of industrial warfare.   The main functions of the councils are to handle grievances; to agree on piece rates, the wage system, and so on, insofar as there is no collective agreement on these matters; to conclude supplementary agreements on wages if the union-sponsored collective agreement authorizes such additional agreements; to be heard or consulted on dismissals or hiring. The council has veto power for certain cases of new hirings; for example, if it claims discrimination "for reasons of race, religion, nationality, origin, political or union activity . . . labor courts have ultimate decision if no agreement can be

---

[15]Heinz Hartmann, "Codetermination in West Germany," *Industrial Relations* 9, no. 2 (February 1970).

reached between the council and management."[16] The council ne-
gotiates work rules such as beginning and end of the work period, timing of vacations, and in-service training. However, as
a rule neither the union nor the council interferes with changes of work methods unless there is a direct impact on employment. Finally—and in many cases most importantly—the council
administers the social welfare agencies of the plant (vacation
homes, kindergartens, credit and relief facilities in emergen-
cies, and so on).

The Works Constitution Law further provides that one-third
of the supervisory board membership of the company consist of
employee representatives, two of whom must be employees of the
firm. They must be elected by all employees in a secret ballot. The representatives are frequently council members. Only
if the supervisory board has nine members or more can there be
employee representatives who are "outsiders." As a result,
boards of nine members or more are not frequent. There is also
an economic committee in larger establishments, half of whose
members are selected by the council, half by management. The
committee members obtain information on economic matters, offer
advice, and are sworn to secrecy.

The system has worked quite differently from the way the
law prescribes. First, many plants have no councils.[17] The
system of consultation on economic matters is often meaningless
—that is, information is provided after the fact, and advice,
when given, is disregarded. The areas in which the councils,
where they exist, seem to be effective concern the details of
working conditions, the setting of piece rates, occasional
grievance handling, and, most of all, the operation of the social welfare institutions of the plant. Complaints about the
failure of the councils to live up to expectations have been
frequent, and the Socialist-led government of Willy Brandt
promised substantial reforms. At the end of 1971 a new Works
Constitution Law was enacted which enlarges the functions of
the Workers Council in many areas, such as the setting of piece
work rates, premium payments, hiring and firing, overtime, etc.
Union access to the plant is guaranteed upon simple notifica-
tion addressed to management.

The main problem for the unions is that under the law the
councils are independent from them and are even sworn to secrecy about many vital business matters. The trade union confederation, aware of this fact, has been consistently asking
for a revision of the law to require the councils to cooperate

---

[16]Sturmthal, *Workers Councils*, p. 63.

[17]In 1963 that proportion was estimated at 20 percent; it is
probably higher today.

with the union in the performance of the councils' tasks. This
has not been accepted so far. Attempts by the unions to bring
their collective bargaining "closer to the plant" have been
only partly successful. As a result of the tight labor market,
as was shown in chapter 6, the gap between contract and effective wages has been wide, to the point that union negotiations
are often without direct relevance for a large number of the
workers covered by the contract. The experience of the 1967
recession, when employers unilaterally cut or eliminated wage
supplements granted in agreements with the councils—such
agreements have no legal standing—was too brief to make a
permanent impact on the system. Employers have consistently
refused to change the nature of agreements and insist upon continued area-wide bargaining. Inevitably the rates set in these
agreements are adjusted to a level acceptable to low-earning
plants. Thus there is ample room for supplements outside the
contract, to be negotiated by the council or by individual employees themselves. The union therefore has limited importance
in the experience of many workers. The unions operate on a far
higher level: they are "administrative" unions. There is also
a generation gap; council members typically belong to the older
generation, whereas the majority of workers has entered the labor force since World War II. This age gap has some ideological connotations. For the older members the union is still
part of a liberating movement, but the younger generation views
the union much more in the spirit of business unionism.

Strangely enough, this generation gap reappears in a very
different way in the relations between the workers and the
councils. "Management and the works council," an astute observer[18] wrote more than a decade ago, "often appear to the
worker as complementary rather than competing institutions. . .
. [It] becomes a harmonizing agency, a sort of buffer between
management and the worker, rather than an organ which takes an
initiative of its own. . . . Wherever codetermination privileges bring members of the works council still more closely together with management . . . a new stratum of industrial func-
tionaries, to some extent sharing management prerogatives,
makes its appearance. The sphere of management may thus tend
to include a privileged upper stratum of the working class."

Complaints that the councils are preventing the union from
operating in the plant, from directly influencing effective
wages, and from handling individual workers' grievances have
become more frequent as the ideological ties between workers

---

[18]Otto Kirchheimer, "West German Trade Unions: Their Domestic
and Foreign Policies," in *West German Leadership and Foreign
Policy*, eds. Hans Speier and W. Phillips Davison (Evanston,
Ill.: Row, Peterson and Co., 1957), pp. 163-64.

and unions have weakened in the last two decades. Some unions have responded by attempting to bring collective bargaining "closer to the plant"—that is, that payments to the workers beyond the rates set in the collective agreement be subject to some general rules agreed to by the union.[19] So far employers have not been ready to make concessions on this issue. Another union effort to bring the union in closer contact with the worker at the work place is the creation of union shop stewards elected by secret ballot by the union members of a plant or of a department in larger plants. They are to handle grievances either directly, if possible, or by transmitting them to members of the council and assisting them in the process. In a few cases enterprises have recognized the shop stewards and extended to them the same rights that members of the council possess, provided the latter designates the shop stewards as council agents.

FRANCE

Labor representatives appear, according to law, in a number of ways in French enterprises. Apart from safety delegates in mines and quarries, who are elected by the workers and are provided with super-seniority, there are shop stewards (délégués du personnel) nominated by "most representative unions" and elected separately for blue-collar and white-collar workers. They handle individual grievances the worker has been unable to resolve with his immediate superior. However, a large number of serious individual grievances tends to be settled in labor courts, which in France have existed since the beginning of the nineteenth century.[20] Because grievances can also be handled by other means—appeals to the government-appointed labor inspectors, who are concerned with the enforcement of labor laws, and to special disciplinary committees in some of the nationalized industries—the role of the shop stewards in grievance handling is not very important. Moreover, the union assists him only in relatively few cases, mainly because of the small number of union officials. Candidates for election to

---

[19]The giant metalworkers' union (I. G. Metall) and the union of workers in the chemical industry (I. G. Chemie) have been among the pioneers in these efforts to change the German bargaining system. In some cases the distance between contract and effective rates has reached 50 percent.

[20]Appeals against decisions of the bipartite labor courts go to the ordinary courts.

the position of the shop stewards are often hard to find, especially in smaller enterprises.

   The plant committees, which go back to the period immediately following the end of World War II, are joint labor-management committees devoted to cooperation between labor and
management.   They are not entitled to engage in bargaining—
although in some cases they have handled individual grievances
—but are to be consulted on matters relating to the organization, administration, and the business policies of the plant.
Two members of the committee are to take part in the meetings
of the board of directors of the enterprise.   The widest authority given to the committees is in the area of the medical
and social services of the plant.   Employers are generally
happy to leave this area to the committees in exchange for
their lack of concern with the technical and business aspects
of the enterprise.   For a long time it seemed that the entire
institution would be reduced to the administration of the social service institutions of the enterprise.   Moreover, the
number of functioning plant committees diminished during the
fifties.

   A reversal of this trend could be observed, however, especially in the latter years of the sixties.   Collective agreements at the plant level made their appearance; informal understandings in which the plant committees or the shop stewards
represented the labor force vis-à-vis management were more frequent.[21]   Yet when the explosion of May-June 1968 occurred, it
demonstrated two contradictory tendencies.   On the one hand,
the events, as they have done many times before, bypassed the
existing insitutions—from the unions, political parties, and
even the government down to the plant committees and shop stewards.   No less important, perhaps, was the revelation of the
powerlessness of employers and employers' associations during
the great crisis.   On the other hand, the main result of the
strikes and demonstrations was the further development of the
same institutions and the fulfillment of long-standing demands
and reform proposals.   Potentially the most important reform
is the introduction of trade union branches in the plants, au-
thorized by a law of December 1968.   Not much is known yet
about whether the French unions are capable of effectively using this opportunity, which existed in some plants even before
passage of the law.

---

[21]See chap. 3, footnote 22.

ITALY

A few comments regarding the role the commissione interni (internal commissions, workers' councils) play in the plants are in order. These are elected representatives of all workers. The lists of candidates are put up by the unions, and the elections are thus a measure of the relative strength of the competitive unions. The main confederations are Communist-dominated (CGIL: Confederacione Generale Italiana di Lavoro), Socialist (UIL: Unione Italiana di Lavoro), and Christian with an admixture of Socialists (CISL: Confederacione Italiana dei Sindacati Liberi). They all tend to maintain union branches in as many plants as possible because they hope thereby to influence the plant elections in their favor. However, these factory cells have played only a minor role in plant-level labor relations.[22] Indeed, it is not quite clear whether two of the major confederations, the CGIL and the UIL, even view the union branches in the plants with much sympathy.

The internal commissions were established by an agreement concluded in 1953 between Confindustria (the top employers' organization) and the three major union confederations; some modifications were introduced in 1966. According to the agreement the commissions are to handle grievances and to supervise the application of the collective agreements. Unions handle grievances only after the commission fails to settle a grievance to its satisfaction and if the complainant is a union member. In the last resort, a court—no special labor courts exist in Italy—may handle the complaint, but a worker may choose to address himself directly to the court, bypassing the commission and the union.

The only confederation which from the beginning attempted to bring about plant-level agreements to supplement the minima set in the national agreements was the CISL. The CGIL at first opposed this plan "as an effort to fragment the working class."[23] Employers too fought the CISL on this issue because they wanted to keep the unions out of the plant. The CISL nevertheless managed to make some progress in concluding plant or company agreements, although the opposition of the employers' confederation frequently forced the union branch to let the

164237

---

[22]*Labor Relations and the Law in Italy and the United States*; a comparative study. Michigan International Labor Studies, vol. 4 (Ann Arbor: University of Michigan Graduate School of Business Administration, 1970), p. 7.

[23]Horowitz, *Italian Labor Movement*, p. 293.

commission sign an agreement the union itself had in fact negotiated.[24]

Thus the CISL, sometimes in cooperation with the UIL, managed to conclude a number of plant agreements without CGIL approval. Such agreements were signed by Fiat, Alfa Romeo, Montecatini, and other companies in 1960 and 1961. The Fiat contract provided increases of 50 to 60 percent above the industry contract level for some wage rates; Alfa Romeo agreed on criteria for incentive pay arrangements; another contract provided for "an almost unprecedented arbitration procedure."[25] In due course the CGIL, fearing that its main competitors might establish themselves firmly in the plants, took greater interest in organizing plant branches, while continuing to stress the role of the internal commissions. The financial weakness of most Italian unions has hindered the development of plant-wide agreements almost as much as the resistance of the employers' organizations and the doubts of the CGIL.

---

[24]Doubts have been expressed as to whether in fact the union branch in the plant negotiated. Arthur Ross thought that it was "rather the district representatives of the national . . . union" ("Prosperity and Labor Relations in Western Europe: Italy and France," *Industrial and Labor Relations Review* 16, no. 1 (October 1962), p. 73.)

[25]Ibid., p. 73.

9

Unions and Nationalization

Nationalization of industrial enterprises has been one of the traditional objectives of the Socialist movements in Europe and of the trade unions associated with the Socialists. However, not all nationalization measures that were enacted were the result of Socialist pressures. Nationalized industries or enterprises existed in various European countries for many years—even centuries—before the rise of a Socialist mass movement. Mercantilistic policies led to government ownership of some enterprises in France; the German railroads have been nationalized practically since they came into being; and in Britain the Port of London, broadcasting, and in some measure the transmission of electrical energy had been nationalized long before World War II. Public ownership in other forms—for example, municipal enterprises—also exists in Europe on a large scale. Nationalization progressed substantially after 1945, and the spirit in which it was undertaken tended to make the role of unions in such industries a problem of significance for the entire labor movement.

Nationalization of industry as viewed by the Socialists must be distinguished from other forms of nationalization. A Syndicalist slogan—which should not be described as nationalization at all—demanding the control of industry by its workers was put forward by some British unions, particularly the miners and the railwaymen, about the time of World War I under the slogan "Workers' Control." French, German, and Austrian labor defined their attitude in favor of nationalization shortly afterward. Little or no action followed these programmatic developments, however. The main impetus for nationalization in Western Europe came after World War II.

The driving force was undoubtedly the increased strength with which labor emerged from the defeat of Hitlerite Germany. The victory of the British Labour party, the advent of Socialists and Communists to power in France and Italy, the return of the Scandinavian labor governments were the outward expressions of this trend. In a number of countries, particularly France, the "collaboration" of big business with the Nazi occupation authorities provided additional reasons for the transfer of business property to the state. The support some businessmen had given to Fascist organizations before the outbreak of the war was regarded by many people even outside the ranks of labor and socialism as evidence of business attempts to defeat the democratic processes. The nationalization of industry would prevent further pressures of organized business interests on the democratically elected government of the country, it was believed. Moreover, wartime controls of the economy, most of which had to be continued into the first postwar years, effectively prepared the ground for nationalization. To progress from a strictly controlled industry to its nationalization was only a minor step and one that many people believed logical. Last, but not least, only the state, with its powers, seemed capable of reorganizing industry after its deterioration during the war and of providing the huge investment funds required.

Nationalization also appeared to be a device that could bring about greater efficiency in industry. As Emmanual Shinwell, a member of the National Executive of the British Labour party, stated at the Forty-fourth Annual Conference of the party in May 1945:

> Certain of our national industries require equipment which will incur huge expenditure. . . . Already the state is being asked to provide finance for industry. In fact, privately owned industry is no longer capable of standing on its own legs. . . . If the capitalist structure in industry has reached such a parlous condition that it can no longer rely on its own resources but must apply to the State for financial assistance, then clearly the State has the right to direct and control and own the industries concerned.

As a consequence a number of substantial nationalization measures were taken in Western Europe, particularly in Great Britain and France, after World War II. To the Port of London and the British Broadcasting Corporation, the Labour government added coal, transport, electricity, gas, cable and wireless, and, finally, after considerable to and fro, steel. Under the leadership of Hugh Gaitskell and, since 1955, Harold Wilson, no further nationalization measures were seriously contemplated. In France nationalization was applied to coal, electricity, and gas, a number of banks and insurance companies, some smaller industries, and a number of individual enterprises, such as the Renault automobile factory, whose main owner and manager had been accused of collaboration with the enemy during the German occupation and had died awaiting trial.

BRITISH UNION POLICY

When shortly before World War I the miners and the railwaymen adopted Syndicalist views, they were clearly at variance
with Labour party policy. For the party introduced—purely for
propaganda purposes—a number of nationalization bills in Parliament which were conceived somewhat along the lines of the
post office. Although the miners' union spread the slogan "The
mines for the Miners!" the Labour party bills provided for the
administration of nationalized industries "by a minister and
his department, tempered by clauses permitting operation by local authorities, or leasing to the previous operators."[1] Because no practical consequences followed from either union
propaganda or Labour party bills, this divergence had no serious effects. A kind of provisional compromise was found in
1918 when the new Labour party program, "Labour and the New
Social Order," and the accompanying resolutions spoke of a
"steadily increasing participation of the workers" in the management of nationalized industries. This was an effort to
reconcile the "efficiency" objectives of the Fabians—Sidney
Webb was the main author of the new program—with the Guild Socialist tendencies of the unions.
Guild socialism in Britain had found its outstanding ad-
vocate in G.D.H. Cole, whose thinking was influenced by French
syndicalism and the ideas of industrial unionism propagated by
the American IWW. Cole's book, *The World of Labour*, first published in 1913 and reprinted a number of times, exerted influence not only in Britain but also elsewhere, primarily by way
of the writings of the Austrian Socialist leader Otto Bauer.
However, although they were influenced by the Syndicalists, the
Guild Socialists rejected outright and full control of industry
by its workers by adding that "the community as a whole must
always reserve an ultimate power to override" the producers'
will.[2] In contrast to the Collectivists and particularly the
Fabians, the Guild Socialists opposed state administration of
industry. This, they feared, would give the government too
much power and would not enable the worker to express his own
personality in his work. Industry should therefore be managed

---

[1]Hugh A. Clegg, *Labour Relations in London Transport* (Oxford:
Basil Blackwell, 1950), p. 4. See also E. Eldon Barry, *Nationalization in British Politics* (Stanford, Calif.: Stanford University Press, 1965); Reuben Kelf-Cohen, *Twenty Years of Nationalization: The British Experience* (New York: St. Martin's
Press, 1969), chap. 11.

[2]G.D.H. Cole, *The World of Labour* (London: G. Bell and Sons,
1913), p. 367.

jointly by the state and the trade unions. Output was to be
determined by the community as a whole, but the actual work
process was to be administered by the unions. This would of
course require a transformation of the unions from a fighting
to an administrative organization. What this meant, in the
miners' view at least, could be inferred from their demand,
addressed to the Royal Commission on the Coal Mines under Sir
John Sankey after World War I, that a majority of the seats in
the district councils, which were to run the mines under a coordinating body, be given to the miners.

Nothing came of this proposal or of the commission in general, but the miners' attitude at that time explains the protest with which many unionists received the London Passenger
Transport Bill worked out by Herbert Morrison during the life
of the second Labour government (1929-31). The bill did not
provide for workers' representation on the board, and its members were to be selected solely on the grounds of competency.
In the discussions that followed, Ernest Bevin, then leader of
the Transport Workers, was Morrison's main opponent. The solution was a compromise in appearance, a defeat of the Guild
Socialists in fact: unions were to have representation on the
boards, but the union officers selected would have to resign
their union office upon appointment and would be responsible
only to the minister.

Once again this was a somewhat academic decision. The Labour government resigned before the London Transport Bill was
passed, and from then until 1940 Labour was in the opposition.
In 1944 the Trades Union Congress published its *Interim Report
on Post-War Reconstruction*, which clearly marked that Morrison
had won over the Guild Socialists. According to the program,
nationalized industries were to be administered by boards appointed by a minister and responsible to him. The board members were to be selected on the basis of competence, but experience gained in the organization of workers should be one of
the desired qualifications. "In the interest of the efficiency
of the industry itself," experienced trade unionists should be
included among the board members. After consulting the appropriate unions, the TUC would submit to the minister a list of
candidates. Upon appointment to the board, the trade unionist
"should surrender any position held in, or any formal responsibility to, the Trade Union." Thus the "viewpoint" of the workers, but not the workers themselves, was to be represented—a
formula widely at variance with the Guild Socialist idea of
"workers' control."

The reasons for this policy were threefold: to be effective in representing the interests of their members, trade unions must retain complete independence from management; trade
unionists who maintained their union status while on the board
would be in an ambiguous position, with loyalties divided be-

tween their constituents and the minister; Parliament, as representative of the entire nation, must have ultimate control over the property of the nation.

The confusion of the issue at this stage was indicated by the facts that this policy was adopted without any lengthy debate and that the Labour party's detailed nationalization proposals on coal, power, and transport continued to refer to workers' participation in the management of nationalized enterprises. But "Let Us Face the Future," the election manifesto of 1945, no longer did so. There could be little doubt that Fabianism had carried the day over Guild Socialism. Even G. D. H. Cole had come to declare that although "the Guild solution is the best in the long run," it would not work satisfactorily at this stage.[3]

POLICY ON THE CONTINENT

The decisive discussion on the Continent occurred immediately after World War I. The most important publication was a series of articles by Otto Bauer in the Viennese Socialist paper, *Arbeiter Zeitung*, which was also published as a pamphlet under the title "Der Weg zum Sozialismus" (The Road to Socialism). Bauer's starting point was similar to that of the Guild Socialists; pure state administration would be dangerous for democracy and inefficient. He proposed instead a "tripartite formula": one-third of the board membership to be elected each by the workers, the consumers, and the state. Consumers' and workers' representatives would defend opposite viewpoints; the representatives of the state would be mediators and arbitrators between them. In his book, *The Austrian Revolution*,[4] Bauer ascribed the origin of his proposals partly to Cole and partly to the lessons he derived from the Russian Revolution.

Bauer's proposals for the organization of nationalized industry were embodied in the Austrian laws on socialization of 1919 and in the German proposal on the coal mines. When the French CGT proceeded in 1919 and 1920 to develop its nationalization program, it dropped the traditional Syndicalist formula in favor of Bauer's tripartite organization, which Léon Jouhaux defended. This system was given the name *industrialized nationalization*. A report of the French Miners Federation of 1920 summarized the ideas of the movement on this issue:

---

[3]G.D.H. Cole, *The National Coal Board*, rev. ed. (London: Fabian Publications, 1949), p. 10.

[4]London: Parsons, 1925.

The organization of the industries to be nationalized must be found by examining all the social interests involved. . . .

One solution only is possible; it is, incidentally, the only one which corresponds to the needs of a good administration; it is to form autonomous organs for every industry in which will take part at the same time the organizations of producers and consumers, as well as the collectivity itself.[5]

These principles have remained unchanged and were applied, although with many variations in detail, when France enacted its nationalization laws after World War II. The boards of the nationalized enterprises have the tripartite composition—although inconsistently—Bauer advocated.

BARGAINING IN NATIONALIZED ENTERPRISES

Two main patterns of nationalization have thus emerged: the British and the French. The first does not include the unions as such in the management of the nationalized enterprises; the second makes them a part of management. Once again we encounter the distinction between "bargaining" and "administrative" unions. The status of the unions in the two systems is different, and from this follow differences in the way wages and working conditions are determined.

In principle the British system is simple. The boards of the nationalized enterprises are employers with whom the unions engage in collective bargaining, very much as they do in their relations with private enterprise. Apart from this bargaining relationship, there exists a system of consultation between management at different levels of authority and the workers. In principle, although not always in practice, the two are kept apart, for the basis of union power is its traditional function of collective bargaining, which must not be sacrificed to the new tasks the union has assumed by consulting with management on the improvement of efficiency. A research group of the Fabian Society stated the reasoning behind this as follows:

One reason for this is that the return of a government hostile to the movement may at any time require it to put forth all its power to resist repressive legislation . . . or to uphold working class stand-

---

[5]Casimir Bartuel (secrétaire général de la fédération), "Rapport sur la Nationalisation des Mines" (Fédération Nationale des Travailleurs du Sous-Sol, 1920).

ards; and even with a friendly government in office,
the trade unions cannot afford to throw away their
weapons of defense. Besides this, in any form of
society, and under any forms of management, workers
will need trade unions to look after their interests
not only in relation to their employers, but also in
relation to the government departments and officials,
and before the courts.[6]

With regard to collective bargaining, therefore, nationalization has introduced few changes. It is true that the duty
of the boards to enter into negotiations with the competent unions is set down in the laws establishing the various nationalized industries,[7] but in nearly all of them, collective bargaining was an accepted practice long before nationalization.
Indeed, the previously existing bargaining machinery has in
most cases been adopted by the boards, although the change of
the structure of the industry did involve a corresponding adap-
tation of bargaining. Thus the new centralized control of labor relations in coal mining or electricity has led to more
uniform wages and working conditions throughout the industry.
Generally this involved "leveling up," but occasionally some
groups lost particular advantages, and this fact has caused a
few conflicts. Undoubtedly wage negotiations in the nationalized industries have a more than ordinary significance. As a
result, although the nationalized industries have a good deal
of independence in the industrial relations field, "major decisions are generally reviewed by the Government."[8]
No uniform system of industrial relations has evolved in
the various nationalized industries, however, and few generalizations can be advanced about them. In several industries negotiations are subdivided for different classes of employees.
Such is the case with electricity, which since 1957 has a complicated organization in which there are five different negotiating bodies. The same applies to the road services, where
three national negotiating committees exist—one for operating

---

[6]Hugh Clegg, *Labour in Nationalized Industry*, interim report of
a Fabian research group, Fabian Research Series 141 (London:
Fabian Society, 1950), pp. 9-10.

[7]The terms used in the Coal Nationalization Act, for instance,
are: "with organizations appearing to them to represent substantial proportions of the persons in the employment of the
Board, or of any class of such persons."

[8]Royal Commission on Trade Unions and Employers' Associations,
Report, 1965-68, p. 33.

personnel, another for maintenance and repair grades, and a separate committee for administrative, professional, and clerical personnel. In coal mining separate agreements have been signed with various classes of employees, all of them fairly similar in structure and providing for three levels of negotiation—pit, district, and national, each having responsibility for problems arising at its own level and those referred to it from a lower level. Wage rates are set nationally, except piece rates, which are determined locally. A frequent feature of agreements in nationalized industries is some form of arbitration, with the award binding on both sides. No legal strike prohibition exists, however,

Although most nationalized industries produced relatively few lasting innovations in the field of industrial relations, a major change occurred in the most prosperous nationalized industry—that supplying electricity. During 1963 "staff" status was offered the industrial employees. This was enacted by stages during the following years, as a result of negotiations between the electricity board and the unions. In essence, "staff" status meant that "all industrial employees were to receive annual salaries instead of hourly rates of pay" and have "the same sick pay benefits as technical and administrative staff." The workers were to cooperate with management "to improve job efficiency and service to the consumer by eliminating overtime working" and by generally working at higher productivity. New arrangements for scheduling working hours were made, combined with a reduction of the work week and longer holidays. The reforms were made gradually over the years following the conclusion of the agreement.[9]

By contrast, industrial relations on the railways are "sad if not tragic," partly because of the unhappy financial situation and a drop in employment on the railroads,[10] but also as a result of a rather sudden shift in wages policy designed to increase productivity. Yet it is unlikely that public funds to cover the huge deficits of the railroads would have been forthcoming as readily as they were without nationalization.[11]

In the field of consultation too developments varied a good deal from industry to industry. The complaint was frequently voiced that managerial personnel were unwilling to engage in sincere consultation and that, in practice, prior noti-

---

[9]Kelf-Cohen, *Nationalization: The British Experience*, p. 258.

[10]Although a similar situation in the coal mining industry— where employment declined between 1957 and April 1968 from 710,000 to 361,000—did not lead to substantial unrest.

[11]Kelf-Cohen, *Nationalization: The British Experience*, p. 264.

fication of impending actions often was substituted for genuine
consultation. Labor representatives were accused of misusing
consultative bodies for bargaining purposes. Dissatisfaction
with the process of consultation led the minister of power to
announce late in 1968 that the consultative machinery in steel,
gas, electricity, and coal was due for investigation and a general overhaul.[12]

FRANCE

The French record of collective bargaining in nationalized
enterprises begins, for practical purposes, in 1950. Between
1945 and 1950, as will be remembered, wages in all industries
were set by the government and even though bargaining was permitted on working conditions little resulted from this authori-
zation. The law of 1950 that allowed collective bargaining on
wages and working conditions has only limited application to
the nationalized enterprises. Under a decree of June 1, 1950,
the main monopolistic public enterprises were exempted from
collective bargaining. Their wages and working conditions continued for many years to be set by law or decree. This group
included coal, electricity, gas, railroads, the Paris Transport
Authority, Air France, and the Banque de France. The other enterprises, including commercial banks and insurance companies
that have been nationalized, come under the agreements covering

---

[12]Because it is widely held in the United States that nationalized industries are less efficient than private enterprise, and
because the evidence produced is usually the deficit of a large
number of them, two considerations need to be kept in mind.
First, in some cases, which welfare economics has discussed at
great length, a deficit may be desirable from the point of view
of general welfare. Second, traditionally "the state has been
landed with many of the most unprofitable estates in the country, in most cases because they have apparently become unwork-
able by anyone else. The full list includes the Sugar Corporation, Cable and Wireless, Ltd., the North of Scotland Hydro-
Electric Board, Short Brothers and Harland, Ltd., the Atomic Energy Authority, and, of course, the Post Office . . ." (Anthony
Sampson, *Anatomy of Britain Today* [New York: Harper & Row, Publishers 1965], p. 571). When Rolls Royce went bankrupt in 1971,
a group of conservative members of Parliament frankly advocated
that the state take the enterprise over, cover the deficit,
make it profitable, and then return it to private enterprise.
This, of course, does not mean that all nationalized enterprises are run efficiently, just as not all private enterprises are
run efficiently.

their industries. Different procedures thus apply to these two groups of public enterprises.

For the first category, whose wages and working conditions were determined by law or decree, bargaining of necessity involved the government. Moreover, the development of a system of "indicative planning"[13] required that both production and wage systems of the nationalized enterprises be fitted into a comprehensive whole—the "plan." This, however, proved difficult and at times impossible.

In the early sixties sharp conflicts in some of the nationalized industries, whose wage levels lagged behind those of private industry, culminated in a miners' strike in March 1963. The government embarked upon an investigation of the wage situation in the coal mines, electricity, gas, Paris transport, and railroads as compared with wages in private industry. The result of this and a subsequent study was the so-called Report Toutée of December 1963, named after the High Court official who chaired the last stage of the investigation. A new wage-setting procedure for the monopolistic sector of the nationalized industries consisted of two stages: (1) The government determines the aggregate wage fund of each of the enterprises and its rate of growth in concordance with the economic plan in force at a given time; the interest groups concerned would be consulted in the process, but no agreement need be established. (2) The distribution of this total within the enterprise would be subject to negotiations with representatives of the personnel. With some modifications this system was adopted in May 1964.[14]

In practice this system was almost never applied, however. One of the many points at issue was how to fit premiums into the scheme. Another difficulty arose out of the failure of the government—for political reasons—to relate the wage increment to the economic plan. However, these difficulties, important as they were, played only a subsidiary role in the fi-

---

[13]A detailed discussion of this system is outside the scope of this investigation. Suffice it to point out that "indicative planning" is an attempt to combine economic planning with the market mechanism. The system endeavors to make the achievement of the planning objectives internally consistent and profitable for private enterprise.

[14]G. Rochecorbon, "Feu la Procedure Toutée?" *Droit Social* 31, no. 11 (November 1968). See also the excellent article by Yves Delamotte, "Recent Collective Bargaining Trends in France," *International Labour Review* 103, no. 4 (April 1971).

nal demise of the system.[15]   The decisive element was the
strike movement of May 1968, which imposed a settlement that
did not correspond to the ideas of the Report Toutée either
in procedure or in content.   It is fair to say that in view
of the wage relationship between the monopolistic nationalized
industries and private enterprise, nationalization holds little appeal for the workers.   That the slogan continues to be
used is the result of tradition far more than of a desire to
extend nationalization.[16]   It is equally significant that after the renationalization of steel was accomplished, the British Labour government has failed to proceed to further nationalization measures.

After the stormy events of 1968 a new system came into
being.   Its first major manifestation was the agreement for
electricity and gas in December 1969.   The new system ties
wage increases to the expansion of the national product, to

---

[15]A study carried out under the chairmanship of S. Nora, submitted in April 1967, pointed at the deficit of the railroads,
and Parisian transport system, and the coal mines, and the
credit needs of electricity and gas.   These were said to endan-
ger the implementation of the fifth economic plan.   See "Groupe
de Travail du Comité Interministeriel des Entreprises Publiques," Rapport sur les Entreprises Publiques, La Documenta-
tion Française, 1967.

[16]One is entitled to doubt," says Reynaud (*Les Syndicats en
France*, p. 192), "whether the workers in the oil refineries are
very eager to orient themselves toward the miners or the railwaymen."

"The basic fact," wrote Anthony Crosland as early as 1956,
"is the large corporation, facing fundamentally similar problems and acting in fundamentally the same way whether publicly
or privately owned.   Its efficiency depends simply on the quality of its top management, and on whether the firm or industry
is structurally well adapted from a technical point of view.
There are, of course, exceptions—as when a dynamic and progressive top management (or an all-important research team) has
a strongly marked private-enterprise outlook, and is very al-
lergic to Whitehall; or where the whole enterprise revolves
round a refractory individual genius; . . . or, in the opposite
case, where the workers would simply refuse to cooperate with
private owners (as they would in coal).   But with these exceptions, ownership as such makes little difference . . . ." (*The
Future of Socialism* [London: Jonathan Cape, 1956, reprinted
1961], p. 480.   The term *Whitehall* stands for government.
Crosland was one of the leading members of the British Labour
government in the sixties.

the performance of the industry, and to changes in the cost-of-living index, with a larger percentage increase to go to lower-paid workers. The unions may substitute shorter hours for wage gains. So-called progress agreements concluded in the other three industries mentioned above provide for a rate of increase of 2 percent per year in real wages. The new system involves the unions in continuous contacts with management and thus in effect gives them higher status and greater responsibilities than ever before.

CIVIL SERVICE

Apart from the nationalized industries, there is the special problem of collective bargaining for the civil service, or to be more precise, for the German *Beamte*, the French *fonctionnaire*, and their equivalents elsewhere. These terms go back to the absolute monarchies of the eighteenth and nineteenth centuries, when the *Beamte* represented the sovereign king.[17] As such he was given special privileges—such as lifetime tenure—but he also accepted unusual obligations extending into his private life. By no means all public employees are civil servants in this sense, even if they perform the same kind of function. Thus about half the German and 80 percent of the Austrian railroad employees are civil servants, whereas in Switzerland all of them are civil servants. Although the non-civil servants are as a rule subject to the same rules in industrial relations as employees of private enterprises, civil servants have their own system, based on the principle that they owe special loyalty, not necessarily to the king, but to the government which is now the successor to the king as the embodiment of sovereignty. Yet a form of quasi-collective bargaining has gradually developed, and civil servants have formed strong unions. Where unionism in general is powerful, the process resembles collective bargaining rather closely, even if under the law the legislatures have final say. In other countries, little more than consultation occurs. In Germany or Austria a process very similar to collective bargaining has evolved. In France the Central Civil Service Committee plays mainly an advisory role.

---

[17]One of the early examples of the legal regulation of this kind of employee is the Prussian Civil Service Code of 1794. See Paul Malles, "Collective Bargaining in the Quasi-Public Sector in Europe," *Canadian Review C.I.R.I.E.C.* (Canadian International Center of Research and Information on Public and Cooperative Economy) 2, no. 2 (July/December 1969), Montreal.

Conciliation or even arbitration machinery exists in a number of countries. Thus in Great Britain a special Civil Service Arbitration Tribunal was set up in 1936, even though the government reserved for itself the right to refuse arbitration "on grounds of policy" in special cases. It has made use of this clause in only one case, however.[18]

The special status of civil servants has gradually eroded during the last twenty years, a process that has gone farthest in Sweden, where the State Service Collective Bargaining Act of 1966 has almost completely abolished the special treatment of civil servants by extending collective bargaining to the civil service.

The relationship between public service employee unions and the labor movement in general varies greatly from country to country. At one extreme is Germany, where the *Beamte* (civil servants in the strict sense of the word) have their own professional organization, independent of both the industrial unions and the white-collar unions. Another pattern of organization is presented by SACO in Sweden, a special federation of academically trained employees in both public and private employment. In the United Kingdom, on the other hand, public service employee unions are affiliated in large numbers with the TUC.

The most delicate issue has been that of the right to strike. In many countries the law is silent on this issue, but in practice civil servants are permitted to strike and have in fact done so. This applies, for instance, to Austria and Belgium. In Sweden the Act of 1966, by applying to civil servants the rules of private industry, has extended to government officials the right to strike and to the government the right to lock out its employees. Norwegian legislation has been interpreted in the same way. France, which has seen some of the biggest public service strikes since World War II, has passed legislation which creates the obligation to give advance notice of strikes and prohibits "rotating" strikes (brief strikes in one department of an enterprise or one enterprise of an industry or area after another). Germany recognizes the right to strike of public employees, with the exception of the civil servants in the narrow definition of the term.[19] However, some general rules apply according to whether or not a dispute is

---

[18]Flanders, *Trade Unions*, pp. 95-96.

[19]In some other countries, for example the U.S. and Australia, strikes in public service are prohibited by law, but this ban seems to be breaking down. Thus the Australian postal service was on strike in 1970 and teachers' strikes have become quite frequent in the U.S.

"contrary to public morals" or if the losses far outweigh
the possible advantages. This may be the case for strikes in
hospitals, public utilities, and public services, especially if
no emergency services are maintained.[20]   This, of course, tends
to make the decision about the legality of a strike uncertain.
In this case and contrary to its legal tradition, Germany turns
to Anglo-Saxon case law. Sweden has a bipartite board whose
function is to prevent or terminate disputes of a "socially
dangerous nature." It is probably fair to say that in this
area of industrial relations—more than almost any other one—
practice and law are widely at variance and are undergoing
rapid change.

---

[20]Malles, "Collective Bargaining," p. 125.

10

Bargaining and Full Employment

A comparison between the non-Communist labor movements
since World War II and their predecessors leads clearly to the
conclusion that the ideological emphasis the earlier movements
possessed has weakened. This is obviously true as far as the
political parties of labor are concerned. Programmatic declar-
ations of some of the leading Socialist parties in Europe contain, as we have seen, few if any references to the class
struggle, the need for the general or even large-scale abolition of private property of the means of production, or other
traditional Socialist objectives. Instead, these parties and
the trade unions inspired by them have adopted programs whose
main planks are full employment, a "fairer" distribution of
the national income, and a highly developed social security
system. Nationalization is increasingly limited to a few key
industries, and even this restricted goal is pursued with less
conviction. In this chapter we deal with the problems full
employment—one of the main objectives of the movement—has
created for the traditional collective bargaining systems.

The fundamental issue is well known and was stated as
early as World War II in the classic Beveridge report on full
employment.[1] When unemployment drops below a certain critical
level for prolonged periods employers' resistance to wage increases tends to weaken; competition for scarce manpower may
induce employers to offer little resistance to workers' demands
or even to improve their own wage rates or other benefits beyond those stipulated in the collective agreements to keep
their existing labor force or to attract additional labor. The
bargaining power of unions and even of individual employees increases. The product market permits employers to transfer increases in costs resulting from wage increases to their custom-

---

[1]William H. Beveridge, *Full Employment in a Free Society* (New
York: W. W. Norton & Co., 1944).

ers, insofar as they are not offset by productivity improvements. Prolonged full employment favors generalized wage increases preceded, followed, or accompanied by corresponding upward price movements. As long as fiscal policy is committed to maintaining full employment and the banking system provides the increased volume of money necessary to finance rising prices and an increased volume of production, the inflationary tendency persists. When the banking system refuses to cooperate, (real) interest rates rise and inflation may reach an end, but so does full employment. In other words, full employment and price stability seem to be incompatible, at least for the long run.

During World War II the government in Great Britain, eager to avoid inflation while mobilization and war production created full employment, applied a policy of mild restraint. Subsidies helped restrain increases in the cost of living, and whatever increases occurred were offset by overtime work, more piecework earnings, and an increase in the number of family members who worked. The unions accepted compulsory arbitration, and only one major strike over wage issues occurred.

During the first postwar years in war-ravaged Europe the issue was seen most frequently in the guise of a balance-of-payments crisis. A general scarcity of goods combined with the breakdown of wartime controls caused rising prices, thus restricting exports and favoring imports. Balance-of-payments crises appeared to be the inevitable consequence of a situation in which imports of raw materials, industrial equipment, and food were vital for reconstruction while production and exports were lagging and monetary reserves were exhausted. Rapid reconstruction was urgently needed, and the contribution of full employment to the payments problem appeared minor. The remedies used were little different from the policies employed during the war except that direct rationing of consumer goods became increasingly difficult to enforce. In the case of Great Britain, for instance, a lagging adjustment of wages to changes in the cost-of-living index and compulsory arbitration of wage claims were the main devices employed. It was hoped that consumption could thus be restrained and imports primarily restricted to items necessary for reconstruction.

Gradually, however, patriotic fervor, which had contributed a good deal to the success of wartime restraints, died down, and the inadequacy of this policy was realized. In the latter part of 1947 it became increasingly difficult to restrain the unions from taking advantage of the favorable situation on the labor market. Moreover, in the interest of reconstruction it became necessary to attract labor into "undermanned" industries such as coal mining, and wage increases became essential for this purpose. These in turn led to wage demands in other industries to maintain "traditional" wage relativities.

An official statement of a new policy appeared early in 1948, when the British Labour government—without prior consultation with the unions—issued a White Paper on "Personal Incomes, Costs and Prices." This document set forth the principles that wage demands should be evaluated according to national objectives, rather than to the desire to maintain or reestablish historical wage relationships. The TUC, while pretending to accept the White Paper, set out four conditions which would make wage increases permissible: (1) increases in output of the industry or trade, (2) substandard wages, (3) the need to attract manpower into essential industries, and (4) "the need to safeguard those wage differentials which are an essential element in the wages structure of many important industries and are required to sustain those standards of craftsmanship, training, and experience that contribute directly to industrial efficiency and higher productivity." This last clause in effect permitted increases of earnings in most industries and contradicted the purpose of the White Paper while seeming to endorse it.

Still, the efforts of the TUC did help to slow the rate of wage increase for a while. Yet it became increasingly obvious that the last clause quoted above offered plenty of opportunities for wage claims that contradicted the government's intentions. Moreover, as time went on, the task of restraining wage demands (demands which employers were quite willing to meet) became more and more difficult for the union leaders. Many unions had cost-of-living escalator clauses in their contracts, and because the index clearly indicated that prices were rising —although at a slower rate—unions were unwilling to forego the advantages the "sliding scales" offered to their members. Moreover, the compression of the wage structure that had occurred during the war caused increasing unrest among the skilled workers. By the end of June 1950 the attempt at generalized wage restraint was abandoned. Bowing to the pressure of the union membership, the General Council of the TUC stated "that there must be greater flexibility of wage movements in the future." The application of this policy "must be left to the good sense and reasonableness which have been displayed by unions, particularly in the postwar period, and with full account being taken of the continued warning of the General Council that our basic difficulties still remain, even if temporarily lessened in their intensity."[2]

---

[2]The record for the index of earnings and of the cost of living in the U.K. and the U.S. for the period from 1935-39 to 1949 shows an almost identical rise in earnings—29 percent in Britain, 30.2 percent for the U.S.—and a higher rise of the cost-of-living index in Britain—78 percent compared with 69.1 per-

The British experience may appear to have been affected by the TUC General Council's lack of control over the collective bargaining activities of the affiliated unions. It may therefore be useful to contrast British developments with those in Norway, a country with a highly centralized union and collective bargaining structure. In Norway, as in Britain, during the war and the postwar years there was a trend toward a compressed wage structure by a relative increase of wages in the lowest-paid occupations; this tendency was created or at least reinforced by flat wage increases to compensate for cost-of-living rises. A wage restraint agreement concluded by the trade union federation in 1946 and extended for another year in 1948 specifically exempted the lowest-paying industries and the lowest-paid workers in general from its restrictions. In contrast to British practices, however, most agreements were concluded by the federation rather than by the individual unions and by the employers' federation rather than by associations of individual industries. In addition, wage boards made awards to the low-paid workers. In this way the unions affiliated with the federation were "discouraged from using their full strength to raise the general standard of their own members irrespective of the position of other groups of workers."[3] The role of a fairly effective price control system and of substantial subsidies to lower food prices should not be neglected either. The heavy dependence of the country on imports—even greater than in the United Kingdom—made the price level only partly a function of Norwegian domestic policy, however.

The main results of this system may be seen in the fact that the cost-of-living index remained stable in 1949 and 1950 while real wages rose. Most of the rise in living costs occurred during the war years, when the index went from 105 (1939) to 160 (1945). From then on the rate of increase was rather low: the index for 1949 was 164. In 1951, however, the Korean War began to have an impact on world prices. Still, compared with Great Britain, Norway's system of highly centralized bargaining lent itself more readily to effective wage restraint.

----

[2](cont'd.) cent in the U.S. At first glance it might appear that British restraint had been rather less successful than U.S. unrestricted bargaining; however, inflationary pressures undoubtedly were more intense in the U.K. after the long years of sharp rationing of consumer goods. On the other hand, the depression of the thirties lasted longer in the U.S. and could have depressed earnings relatively more than in the U.K.

[3]L. Inman, *Post-War Wages Policy in Norway*, Bulletin of the Institute of Statistics (Oxford) 12, nos. 7-8 (July-August 1950).

In both cases one of the keys to this policy was the willingness of union leadership to engage in self-restraint, a policy
dictated at least partly by political considerations. In both
countries a labor government was in office during the period
under review, and the unions were willing to make sacrifices
for the sake of the political party with which they were associated. The figures quoted above indicate that this effort was
not completely unsuccessful, yet they also suggest that labor
operated under an illusion and that there were fairly narrow
limits to the effort.

The central illusion was that in some way the inflationary
trend was merely the result of the war and the extreme shortages created by it. Once postwar reconstruction was completed
—a somewhat loosely defined objective—restraints could be
removed. The Korean War, which produced worldwide shortages of
goods, was held responsible for the postponement of the "return
to normalcy" in collective bargaining. The fact that long-term
full employment would tend to fundamentally change the whole
climate of collective bargaining, as Beveridge had pointed out,[4]
was only gradually and reluctantly perceived.

The delay and perhaps reluctance to confront the implications of full employment for the traditional industrial relations system is perhaps best illustrated by the failure of all
but a few Western nations to examine the Swedish experience of
the "wages slide." In that country, for patriotic reasons as
well as out of consideration for the Social Democratic government, the unions attempted in 1949 and 1950[5] to exert a strict
control over wage developments in order to prevent inflationary
price movements. Their efforts were crowned with less than
complete success, as a result mainly of a phenomenon until then
little understood in industrial relations analysis. The unions
exerted self-restraint in wage demands, contracts avoided all
increases, and the government used subsidies to keep the cost
of living as close as possible after a currency devaluation in
1949. Yet employers, confronted with extreme labor shortages,
outbid each other beyond the contract terms to attract or to
retain the labor force they needed. Earnings thus rose faster
than provided in the contracts. This phenomenon, called *wages
slide* or *wages drift*, put the unions in the embarrassing posi-

---

[4]*Full Employment.*

[5]Prior to this, between 1945 and 1948, unions bargained indi-
vidually on the basis of general recommendations of the confederation (LO) in favor of more generous treatment for the lowest-
paid workers. T. L. Johnston, *Collective Bargaining in Sweden:
A Study of the Labor Market and Its Institutions* (Cambridge:
Harvard University Press, 1962), p. 279.

tion of attempting—unsuccessfully—to prevent their members
from obtaining wage increases which some employers, especially
those in capital-intensive firms or industries, were willing to
grant. Obviously no labor union can long demand membership
loyalty and dues for that purpose. The Swedish experiment in
union wage restraint thus ended in failure, at about the same
time that the British unions withdrew from their attempt.

This failure was a beginning rather than an end, however.
It became increasingly clear as time went on that postwar scarcity of goods and the requirements of reconstruction no longer
created the inflationary problems. Nor was the problem excess
demand for goods and services, as in former inflations, although this phenomenon also occurred. Rather, the cause of inflation was the persistence of full employment. Moreover, although public opinion tended to hold the unions responsible for
inflation, investigations in a variety of circumstances indicated that even in the absence of unions and of collective
agreements the phenomenon of rapidly rising wages in excess of
productivity increases occurred whenever full employment existed for long periods. Indeed, it has never been clearly established whether, given full employment, unions speed up—by
greater market power—or delay—by the conclusion of long-term
agreements—the process of wage-induced inflation or whether
they have little influence on increases of labor costs.

From about the middle of the fifties on, new attempts were
made to combine full employment, price stability, and free collective bargaining. It soon developed that the three elements
in this "magic triangle" were not compatible. Indeed, balance-
of-payments problems—no longer related to the difficulties of
postwar reconstruction—added a fourth element, equally difficult to fit into the puzzle. Attempts at effecting a compromise solution among these objectives were made under labels
ranging from "income policies" to "guideposts" and "concerted
action," all of which were, in effect, mild forms of wage (and
usually price) control.

Most non-Communist unions did not oppose such policies;
however, they tied their acceptance to a number of conditions,
primarily that controls or guidelines not be limited to wages
but cover nonwage incomes and prices as well. To trade union
leaders who rejected such government intervention outright, the
advocates of incomes policies responded that in any case governments intervene in income distribution by way of fiscal policies. A negotiated wage increase, for instance, can be frus-
trated or reversed by government tax policies.[6] Price controls

---

[6]Derek Robinson, as quoted in "Labor Developments Abroad" (Bureau of Labor Statistics, U.S. Department of Labor, June 1967),
p. 13.

were advocated in preference to profit controls, in order not to weaken the incentive for efficiency. Wage flexibility was believed unnecessary as a tool for labor mobility, at least in the short run.[7]

We cannot explore in detail the problems of various forms of incomes policies in different countries at different times. Moreover, *incomes policies* is the label for a whole class of varied policies that have a common objective: to restrain the increase of prices by restricting the rise of wages and other cost items under conditions of full employment. Protagonists of such policies tend to present their views in different ways, so that sweeping generalizations can always be met by references to exceptions, and often explain the rationale of the policy in opposite ways. As one example, the Report of the Royal Commission on Trade Unions and Employers' Associations (the Donovan report) described incomes policies as "concerned with the short-run improvement of the country's economic position." At the same time Aubrey-Jones, the chairman of the British National Board of Prices and Incomes, claimed that "the essential case for the policy rests . . . less on its short-term usefulness than on its long-term need."[8] Nor was there agreement on the relationship of incomes policies to the traditional devices of fiscal and monetary policy in the combined policy system designed to achieve maximum price stability in a society of full employment. The traditional view regarded incomes policies as auxiliary to the monetary and fiscal steering devices. Others pointed out that monetary policy was "increasingly used to influence international movements of short-term capital"[9] rather than to stabilize domestic prices, whereas fiscal policy, compelled to rely more and more on indirect taxes, would tend to increase prices and have an uncertain impact on saving/spending ratios. The ultimate effect on the price level could not be predicted with any certainty. Direct intervention in the mechanism of wage and price fixing was thus described as the only reliable way to assure price and cost stability.

The record of incomes policies when maintained over longer periods is hardly encouraging, however. The British experience after the collapse of the White Paper policy in 1950 is instructive. In 1956 a Conservative government induced the employers to pledge a united front against wage increases. In

---

[7]See *Wages and Labor Mobility* (Paris: OECD, July 1965).

[8]"Prices and Incomes Policy," *The Economic Journal* 78, no. 312 (December 1968): 800.

[9]Ibid., p. 801.

the spring of 1957 strikes in the metal (engineering) and ship-building industries forced the employers to give way, on the government's urging. Fear that a new balance-of-payments crisis would result from the strikes played a large role in the failure of this attempt.

In 1961 the government made a new attempt by announcing a "pay pause" to be applied "in all areas under government control—in the civil service, in the health service, in the nationalized industries, and in private industries covered by statutory wage legislation."[10]   Private employers were asked to cooperate, but the unions refused. As far as government influence reached the pause was effective; elsewhere the attempt was less successful. It lasted only eight months. This radical measure was followed by an attempt to keep pay rises in line with productivity increases, in the hope of stimulating economic growth. This attempt too failed by almost universal disregard, culminating in the universities' offer of "the most generous pay increase that University teachers have ever received."[11]

The Labour government that took office in 1964 came in with the deliberate purpose of instituting an incomes policy with which unions and employers would agree. Productivity increases were to be fostered by the policy, and it was to be administered by a high-powered National Board for Prices and Incomes. Almost every conceivable variation of the basic themes—ceilings on wage, price, and dividend increases, delays in such increases, tradeoffs between wage and productivity increases, and so on—were tried between 1964 and 1970. The end of the experiments was indicated when the rate of wage increases in the last months of 1969 and early 1970 often vastly exceeded the rules laid down in government policy statements and the Prices and Incomes Board was frequently bypassed in important decisions.

One of the main factors in the failure of the experiments was once again the phenomenon of *wage drift*, or the difference between contract rates and effective earnings. This gap consists mainly of three elements. Perhaps the most important of these is the system of piece rates or incentive pay. In the normal course of events, as their experience grows piece-workers enjoy growing earnings, even if rates remain unchanged. Second, overtime earnings at rates above those of the standard working hours add to weekly earnings. In many cases workers benefited from guaranteed overtime, whether it was actually

[10]Hugh Clegg, *How to Run an Incomes Policy and Why We Made Such a Mess of the Last One* (London: Heinemann, 1971), p. 2.

[11]Ibid., p. 3.

worked or not.[12]   And third, pay supplements to the contract
rate are negotiated in the firm or plant. As a result, controls over contract rates may help little or not at all in restraining effective earnings, which matter from the point of
view of both labor costs and effective demand.

THE DUTCH EXPERIMENT

Problems of a different kind, added to some of those just
described, emerged in the course of Dutch incomes policy, which
was the most consistent attempt to resolve the problem in what
was regarded as a scientific way. Arising out of the resistance movement and the cooperation of unions and employers
against the German occupation forces, several variations of
controls of wage levels and of determining wage relationships
were introduced successively after the war. The main elements
in this system were the Foundation of Labor and the Board of
Mediators. The first was a joint organization of management
and labor which permitted cooperation among the various ideologically and religiously divided trade union confederations
and the employers' organizations. The Board of Mediators was
an official agency that handled wage issues in the last resort.
Job evaluation was to provide scientific guidance for determining wage relationships, and measurements of productivity changes were to perform the same service for changes in the general
wage level. At first the controls quite successfully delayed
the progress of inflation during the reconstruction period and
until late in the fifties. However, the tightening domestic
labor market and the increasing absorption of Dutch manpower by
the prospering economy in neighboring Germany led to increasingly frequent violations of the system. "Black wages," secret
illegal arrangements by which employers paid higher wages than
were approved by the government-sponsored Board of Mediators,
in the end defeated the controls.

By 1961 it was becoming obvious that major changes in
wages policy were unavoidable. Attempts to prevent the inevitable failed. After various experiments, an agreement between
the unions and the employers' federations in 1967 decided that
government intervention would be limited to cases in which the
minister of labor decided within three weeks of the conclusion
of an agreement that the wage terms would have an unsettling
effect on the economy as a whole. This was accepted by the
government in 1968, but events made public regulation of wage

---

[12]"Some regularly earn ten, fifteen or even twenty hours' overtime pay a week" (Clegg, *How to Run an Incomes Policy*, p. 5).

changes increasingly difficult to enforce.[13]   In 1970 the Board
of Mediators was dissolved; the cornerstone of the formerly
strict Dutch wages policy was abandoned.

FRENCH PLANNING

French "indicative planning" offered another example of an
attempt at an incomes policy in a country with a tight labor
market. The fact that important French industries are nationalized added special features to this experiment and one of the
early attempts at formulating an incomes policy originated in a
strike in the nationalized coal mines during the winter of
1963–64. A committee studied the situation and came to the
conclusion that the annual rate of increase of the wages fund
of each nationalized enterprise, assuming unchanged employment,
should be determined by the government on the basis of the national economic plan. The distribution of this total should be
left to negotiations between unions and management in each enterprise. For the private sector, elaborate discussions led to
a report by Pierre Massé, then the top planning official of the
country. He proposed that guidelines combine the criteria of
overall and sectoral productivity increase in some fashion and
that the guidelines concern profits as well as wages. No official commitment to this policy could be obtained from any of
the union centers, each of whom gave different reasons for its
refusal; nor did the government carry out all the Massé proposals for the implementation of the policy suggested in the report. Indeed, in practice only the report on incomes policies
in the public sector played any significant role—the automobile firm Renault excepted—and the entire system broke down in
the violent upheavals in France in 1968.

WEST GERMANY

In a somewhat inconspicuous manner West Germany is pursuing an incomes policy, called *concerted action*, in the form of
conferences among government, union, and employers' association
representatives and experts. For most of the post–World War II
period Germany combined rapid economic expansion with remarkable price stability, due to a set of special circumstances.
The immigration of millions of German-speaking refugees from
Eastern Europe, which at first was mainly regarded as a heavy
burden on the scarce resources of the war-devastated country,

---

[13]John P. Windmuller, *Labor Relations in the Netherlands*
(Ithaca, N.Y.: Cornell University Press, 1969).

proved a blessing in disguise in the rapidly expanding economy, as did the recruitment of hundreds of thousands of foreign workers, mainly in Italy but also in Spain, Turkey, Greece, and Yugoslavia. Another factor was a high degree of self-restraint on the part of the unions, whose members were willing to contribute toward rebuilding the country. The workers accepted relatively low real wages during the first postwar decade and even beyond it, as long as the twin dangers of inflation and unemployment could be avoided. At the same time the members of the employers' associations maintained strict discipline in dealing with the workers, a form of class consciousness and class solidarity that survived all social and political changes in the country. Under the slogan "social market economy" the post-World War II German governments relied on these self-regulatory factors rather than direct government intervention in the market.

In the early sixties the amazing recovery of the country put a severe strain on union discipline. The largest of the German unions, the I. G. Metall (metalworkers' industrial union) under the leadership of Otto Brenner, began a more aggressive wages policy. This was stimulated, at least in part, by the widening gap between contract and reality—that is, between the rates set in the contracts and the consistently higher earnings resulting from supplements granted in the plants under the pressure of the tight labor market. Before the full impact of this change could be felt, economic and political events radically altered the entire framework within which the unions operated.

A severe if short recession in 1966-67 ended the neoliberal policy of the government and the political career of its main protagonist, Ludwig Erhard. The Social Democratic party (SPD) entered a government coalition with the Christian Democrats (CDU), and the new minister of economic affairs, Karl Schiller (SPD), successfully introduced Keynesian policies to overcome the recession. To counteract the inflationary tendencies which the achievement of exceedingly low unemployment rates threatened to bring about, he relied first on Keynesian fiscal policies—now used in reverse—and an upward move of the currency exchange rate. The next step was concerted action —that is, the cooperation of employers' associations, unions, government, and experts, testing the ability of the interest groups to keep their members in line to restrain price and wage increases. The new policy worked for some time with remarkable success, first setting an end to the recession and then moderating the price increase that accompanied the return to full employment. Compared with most other industrial nations, West Germany managed to keep the rate of increase of the cost of living remarkably low. Yet a considerable price had to be paid for this success.

By cooperating with the government and the employers in
the informal process of concerted action, the union leaders
hoped to have the best of both worlds: to be accepted as full
partners with employers and the government in influencing important aspects of economic policy while avoiding the open responsibility the formal acceptance of "guideposts" or of other
official incomes policy might have involved.

This strategy did not operate successfully for long. In
1969 wildcat strikes broke out in shipbuilding, steel, coal
mining, and the textile industries and in most cases led to
almost unbelievably rapid success for the workers. The capitulation of the employers in the face of this unexpected onslaught of the traditionally disciplined German workers left
the union leadership in a dangerously exposed position. Not
only the future of concerted action but the entire system of
German collective bargaining were questioned. In a rapid response the unions announced that their participation in concerted action in the future would be based on their own estimates of the rate of wage and salary increases compatible with
economic expansion under conditions of stable prices rather
than those of the government or of experts. In the chemical
industry the union demanded collective bargaining at the level
of the enterprise to reduce or even eliminate the gap between
the rates set in area-wide agreements and effective rates.
This demand, following on persistent efforts of the metalworkers to bring collective bargaining "closer to the plants," appeared to many observers to mark the beginning of a process
that might lead to fundamental reexamination of the German industrial relations system and perhaps that of other Western
nations as well.

The German wildcat strikes of 1969 and their lightning
successes were only part of a wider movement that extended to
Britain, France, Italy, and Sweden. Although wildcat strikes
have been a feature of the British industrial relations scene
for many years, the almost explosive transfer of rank-and-file
militancy to the Continent since 1968 represented a new depar-
ture. The new militancy—often under the leadership of shop
stewards—was directed against union leaders almost as much as
against the employers.

One of the bases for the protest is the structure of the
unions. The failure of most European unions to develop an effective union organization in the plant, combined with the
handling of workers' grievances by shop stewards elected by all
workers and thus not always owing primary loyalty to the union,
has created a feeling of alienation between workers and union
leaders. The leaders appear all too often as part of what it
has become fashionable to call the power structure. As unionism has become accepted in the Western world, union leaders
have become part of the "establishment."

The gap between union leaders and the rank and file results from the union structure itself and is thus of long
standing. What has made this issue explosive is the presence
of long-term full employment and the attempt to use the unions
as instruments of wage restraint. To try to make full employment compatible with a high degree of price stability is of
course a praiseworthy attempt. To do so by using the unions
as means of wage restraint, not merely for a temporary emergency but for the long run, however, seems doomed to failure.
True, some union structures lend themselves more readily to
the enforcement of wage restraint than others. In general,
the more centralized the bargaining system, the more removed
union leadership is from the rank and file, and the more incor-
porated the unions are into the government structure—for example, by way of a labor party in government—the less are the
difficulties of an incomes policy. Yet merely listing these
characteristics indicates the difficulties for the long run.
First, union members can hardly be expected to pay dues to
maintain organizations whose purpose is to try to prevent union members from obtaining wage increases which in tight labor
markets employers are often willing to grant. For a short-term
national emergency patriotism may allow union leaders to act
against the immediate interest of their members on the understanding that the labor organizations will resume their normal
operations—which aim at raising the incomes of their members—
as soon as the emergency is over. If full employment is to
persist for long periods, however, it cannot be treated as if
it were a short-term emergency.

Second, experience everywhere indicates that the enforcement of an incomes policy aiming at wage restraint is exceedingly difficult. Wages drift—a rise in earnings above the
level called for in the collective agreement—is a phenomenon
almost universally observed where long-term wage restraint has
been attempted in a tight labor market. Its various elements
have already been referred to. To this list should be added
the payment of "black wages," as it occurred in the Netherlands. No organization in a reasonably free society is efficient enough to ferret out all or even a substantial part of
the cases in which wages drift represents a violation of the
rules set under a policy of wage restraint.

Third, the unions seem especially ill equipped to become
the policemen of wage restraint. Not only does the assignment
run counter to their basic purpose but their means of ascer-
taining and preventing cases of violation are inadequate, especially in the frequent situation in which the union does not
operate in the plant. The employer alone knows the actual
earnings of all of his employees, and if enforcement is to be
effective, the employer rather than the union would have to be
its agent.

Finally, long-term wage restraint requires in practice, though not necessarily in principle, that everyone concerned— employer, union, worker, other social groups—accept a given income distribution as fair and reasonable and consequently make no attempt to change it, even if circumstances would permit him to do so. This is unlikely to occur in the foreseeable future. Therefore, no real solution to the problems created by long-term full employment is in sight.[14] Conceivably, none is possible within the existing social framework. Capitalism plus long-run full employment is perhaps a quite different animal from the social system existing before World War II. We may have to be satisfied with accommodation by trading off some degree of inflation against some measure of unemployment and less stable exchange rates. The more elastic supply curves of labor we can develop, the easier accommodation will be. The advance of new manpower and education policies, together with the removal of institutional barriers to labor and capital mobility, may be the most promising road to pursue for a long time.

However, political pressures may force governments into experiments with various forms of wage and price restraints of a more or less stringent nature. If pressures are strong, the restraints may prove effective for relatively short periods. At a minimum they may provide temporary political relief for a government in distress. Few experts will assert, on the basis of international experience, that they represent a solution to a long-term—or even a medium-term—problem, however.

---

[14]"The task of combining prosperity with price stability now stands as the major unsolved problem of aggregative economic performance" (Arthur M. Okun, *The Political Economy of Prosperity* (Washington, D.C.: The Brookings Institution, 1970), p. 130).

Part Three

11

The International Labor Movement

The following three chapters are devoted to problems that go beyond the geographical limits of Western and Central Europe. They deal briefly with the international labor organizations (especially their relationships with U.S. labor), labor in developing countries, and the industrial relations systems of the countries that claim adherence to the principles of socialism. We look first at the rise of international labor organizations.

Because the labor movements in most European countries originated as primarily political organizations, a separate international trade union organization developed late: it came into being only at the beginning of this century. Until then international trade union gatherings took place in connection with international Socialist congresses. Socialist trade unionists who were delegates to these congresses met for an afternoon or two to exchange information and experiences. International Trade Secretariats, which combined unions of the same craft or industry in a number of countries, appeared somewhat earlier. The typographical unions—pioneers of the labor movement in many countries—were the first to establish their international association. They met for that purpose in 1889, in conjunction with the founding congress of the (Second) Socialist International.[1] The miners and other unions followed their

---

[1]The International Workingmen's Association (also called the First International) was founded in 1864 in London. Karl Marx was its guiding spirit. The "Inaugural Address of the International" written by Marx culminated in the sentences: "To con-

example, until early in this century some thirty such international trade secretariats existed, usually administered by one
of the affiliated unions. More than two-thirds of the trade
secretariats had headquarters in Germany, a sign of the relative affluence and the high standing of the German unions before World War I.

A main achievement of the Second Socialist International
was the establishment of the First of May celebration. American trade union delegates present at the founding congress reported that the AFL had called for workers' demonstrations in
favor of the eight-hour working day and had set the date for
these demonstrations—the First of May 1890. Because the congress was anxious to arrange working-class demonstrations in
all countries on one given day as a symbol of international
labor solidarity, the date already set by the Americans was
adopted as the universal date. The First of May demonstrations, now often regarded erroneously as a Communist symbol,
are thus of American origin.

An international trade union organization that cut across
occupational and industry lines did not exist until 1901. Even
then the newly established International Secretariat of National Trade Union Centers was intended merely as a small auxiliary
body attached to the Socialist International. The latter was
recognized as the leading international representative of the
workers. The new International Trade Union Secretariat was attached to the German trade union center, which provided the
modest services of mutual information that the International
Trade Union Secretariat was intended to perform.

The main resistance to subordination of the unions to the
Socialist International came at first from the French and later
from the Americans. The French Syndicalists opposed the Socialist International for ideological reasons. They wanted to
see established a full-fledged international trade union organization to discuss such favorite Syndicalist topics as antimil-
itarism and the general strike as a revolutionary weapon. The
great majority of trade unionists, however, viewed these subjects as belonging to the competency of the political organization. The American unions joined the nascent International
Trade Union Secretariat after Samuel Gompers made a trip to Europe in 1909, even though he was aware of the profound ideolog-

---

[1](Cont'd.) quer political power has . . . become the great duty
of the working class. . . . One element of success they possess
—numbers; but numbers weigh only in the balance if united by
combination and led by knowledge." In later years the influence of Anarchists led by Bakunin grew within the International
and led to its demise. A new organization arose under Socialist control in 1889.

ical differences separating the AFL from its European colleagues. Gompers hoped to move the European trade unions in
the direction of business unionism. He thus joined the French
in opposing the alliance with the Socialists, although for different reasons.

Under the combined pressure of the French and the Americans, but also as a result of the growing self-confidence of
the unions, the International Secretariat was reorganized in
1913 as the International Federation of Trade Unions (IFTU).
It operated with a minimum of rules. Each affiliated national
center was free "to determine its own tendency and tactics,"
but only one center from each country could be affiliated.
This clause prevented the affiliation of the Czech unions,
whose rising nationalism caused them to sever their relations
with the Austrian center in the Hapsburg monarchy; this clause
also kept out the Christian trade unions that had come into
being in several Continental countries around the turn of the
century. The total membership affiliated with the IFTU before
World War I was 7.4 million. One-third came from Germany; the
AFL provided the second largest contingent.

Relations between the AFL and the IFTU were far from happy. From the beginning of the American affiliation Gompers
objected to the Socialist influence on the IFTU and to the
revolutionary Syndicalist leanings of the French. The friction came to a head during World War I. Gompers objected to
the organization of "Allied Socialist and labor conferences,"
not only because they officially combined delegates of Socialist parties and of trade unions from the Western Allies, but
also because of the growing influence of pacifists and inter-
nationalists within these conferences. Gompers himself was a
staunch supporter of official American war policy and a committed opponent of internationalist and pacifist views. Gompers
attended the congress in 1919 in Amsterdam, when the IFTU was
reconstituted in an atmosphere of radicalism created by the
revolutionary events following the end of the war, but shortly
afterward the AFL withdrew. In its view the IFTU was committed
"to a revolutionary principle, to which the American Federation of Labor is and always has been uncompromisingly opposed
and to which no labor movement guided by democratic ideals
could give approval."[2]

Yet relations between American and European trade unionists were not completely severed. The AFL continued to send
fraternal delegates to the annual meetings of the British
Trades Union Congress. Later, when the U.S. joined the International Labor Organization (ILO), which came into being after

---

[2]Samuel Gompers, *Seventy Years of Life and Labor* (New York:
E. P. Dutton & Co., 1943), p. 509.

World War I—to a large extent as a result of Samuel Gomper's work at the Versailles Peace Conference—new ties were formed between the trade unions on both sides of the Atlantic. The ILO was designed to improve the living standards of working-class people and to reduce international competition based on exploitation of labor. It introduced a new organization principle in official international cooperation. The national delegations to the annual ILO conferences consist of two government delegates and one delegate each from employers and trade unions. The AFL designated the American labor delegate; most European workers' delegates represented organizations affiliated with the IFTU. The ILO conferences, usually held at the seat of the organization in Geneva, Switzerland, thus offered regular opportunities for AFL leaders and European trade unionists to meet.

More important at the time than the break with the AFL was the Communist onslaught on the IFTU. The Communist International (Comintern), established in the wake of the Bolshevik Revolution in Russia, exerted for a while a powerful influence on the workers on the European continent. Strengthened by the prestige of the victorious Red Army, the Comintern set down twenty-one requirements for affiliation. One of them demanded that all Communists wage war "against the yellow Amsterdam International."[3] Moreover, in 1921 the Communists organized their own trade union international, the Red International of Labor Unions (Profintern). Its first assignment was to take control of the unions by "boring from within" that is, by organizing Communist factions within the unions. Later Communist-controlled unions were created in some countries. These attempts enjoyed only temporary success, but a potential threat to the Socialist control of unions remained. After World War II Communist-dominated unions became a major factor in a number of countries, especially France and Italy.

Shortly before the outbreak of World War II relations between European and American unions greatly improved, although some of the reasons for this change were somewhat peculiar. The AFL returned to the IFTU when the possibility arose that the newly founded CIO would be admitted to the international trade union body. In a hard-fought battle the AFL succeeded in obtaining affiliation for itself, thus blocking the affiliation of the CIO (the statutory limitation of one affiliate from each country still existed).

During World War II, however, the international influence of the Russian unions and of the CIO grew to the point that an attempt was made to combine American, European, Russian, and

---

[3]The term *yellow* in labor parlance is roughly equivalent to "employers' agent."

other unions in one international association. The reasons
were mainly related to the war: Russia was an ally of the West,
and the CIO was strongly entrenched in war-essential industries
in the U.S. The AFL refused to cooperate, however, and the
British TUC was only reluctantly drawn into the organization.
For a short time the mood generated by the wartime alliance
prevailed, and with the cooperation of the CIO the World Federation of Trade Unions (WFTU) was born in 1945, while the IFTU
was officially dissolved. This attempt at an East-West understanding among trade unions lasted as long as the governments
on both sides cooperated. The announcement of the Marshall
Plan for the reconstruction of Europe led to an open break.
The leading non-Communist unions withdrew from the WFTU, and
the International Trade Secretariat, led by non-Communist unions, declared open war upon it. At the same time the non-
Communist wing of the French trade unions broke with the Communist-controlled trade union center, the CGT, and set up its
own organization, CGT-Force Ouvrière. Late in 1949 the non-
Communist trade union centers met in London to create a new
trade union international, the International Confederation of
Free Trade Unions (ICFTU).

The conference consisted of delegates from fifty-three
countries representing fifty-nine national centers and twenty-
eight individual unions—altogether some 48.5 million organized
trade unionists. Another million and a half workers were represented by observers. Although not all of these official membership figures can be accepted with equal confidence, the IC-
FTU undoubtedly was and remains the strongest international
trade union organization outside the Communist sphere of domination.

Two main features characterized the new organization—one
organizational, the other ideological. In order to accommodate
the American unions still split into the AFL and the CIO, the
ICFTU dropped the traditional clause restricting membership to
one trade union center from each country. Both American centers and even an unaffiliated U.S. union—the United Mineworkers—were admitted to membership. Indeed, an invitation was
addressed to Christian trade unions to affiliate, provided only
that they dropped their affiliation with the small International Federation of Christian Trade Unions (IFCTU).

Ideologically—as this move may indicate—the new organization was united more in a negative than an affirmative program. Anti-Communism was the one tie that held the affiliates
together. Within this frame their ideologies ranged from mild
forms of democratic socialism to support of a reformed capitalism. Common positive programs were thus difficult to develop,
and the language used in the resolutions of the ICFTU was a
carefully devised compromise between the American emphasis on
free private enterprise and the language of the Europeans,

whose traditional Socialist orientation was just beginning to
undergo substantial changes. With U.S. membership representing
by far the strongest single national bloc within the organization, the accommodation made considerable allowances for the
American views. The gradual development of regional organizations—especially a European grouping and the Regional Organization for the Western Hemisphere (ORIT: Organizacion Regional
Interamericana de Trabajadores)—served for a while to separate
the differing viewpoints. The administrative machinery, with
its headquarters in Brussels, Belgium, and a general secretary
selected from a small country, was designed to facilitate compromise solutions. Yet in due course the divergencies between
the members on the two sides of the Atlantic Ocean severely
tested the limits of tolerance of the organization.

The differences between the American and the European
views were many. They related not only to ideological issues
but also to styles of unionism, the personalities of the leaders, the material means at the disposal of various national
centers, and many issues of policy and methods of operation.
One of the main sources of disagreement was the international
activities individual affiliated organizations carried on,
sometimes in competition with each other and often to the neg-
lect of the financially less well-equipped ICFTU. The AFL-CIO,
in cooperation with ORIT and also with U.S. employers, organized the American Institute for Free Labor Development (AIFLD),
which conducts educational, training, and social development
programs in Latin America. Similarly, the AFL-CIO African-
American Labor Center (AALC), is engaged in various activities
in Africa, and another group operates in Asia. Other national
centers, notably the British TUC, the West Germans by way of
the Friedrich Ebert Foundation, and, a latecomer, the Swedish
trade union federation (LO: Lands-Organisationen) are also undertaking educational and related activities in developing
countries. These separate activities have tended to overshadow
the ICFTU effort in these areas, which has been the cause of
friction between the international organization and its major
affiliates who dispose of far larger resources than the ICFTU.
There are good reasons to believe that some of these activities
are at least partly—sometimes very largely—supported by the
respective governments. Of the friction created by these often
competitive activities, C. V. Devan Nair, of the Singapore National Trades Union Congress, said at the ICFTU Congress in
1969: "Any substitution of genuine, bona fide international activities in the developing world, through an international instrument like the ICFTU, by an unholy multitude of competing
and rival national initiatives, must, perforce, willy-nilly,
lead to what is known as 'balkanization'." An apparent compromise was achieved at the ICFTU Congress in 1965, when it was
decided that the international organization should act as a

coordinating body for all bilateral programs, but in fact this
decision merely put the stamp of approval on the existing state
of affairs.

No less serious was an almost uninterrupted series of disagreements between the AFL-CIO and the Secretariat of the ICF-
TU, which enjoyed the support of most of its European affiliates. Although the bulk of the American union membership cared
little about the international activities of labor, most of the
leaders viewed the ICFTU primarily—some perhaps almost exclu-
sively—as an instrument in the struggle against communism.
Most of the European laborites, although clearly anti-Commu-
ist, pursued the struggle against the WFTU and its Communist
allies with somewhat less than single-minded devotion, or at
least with different methods than those of the AFL-CIO leaders.
The latter officially and categorically rejected all contacts
with what they described as the bogus labor organizations in
the East; European unions made repeated, although not usually
successful, attempts to reduce friction with the labor organizations of their Communist neighbors. Inevitably the ICFTU was
drawn into the ensuing conflict between European unions and the
AFL-CIO. With deadly monotony one general secretary of the IC-
FTU after another fell victim to this divergence of views. Internal ideological and personal friction in the United States—
especially between George Meany and Walter Reuther, the presidents of the AFL-CIO and the United Auto Workers (UAW)—added
fuel to the fire because one of the issues in their conflict
concerned international problems: Walter Reuther had considerably more understanding for the European labor strategy than
Meany. In 1968 the UAW withdrew from the AFL-CIO and in due
course asked for admission to the ICFTU as a separate organization. Precedents for multiple affiliations from one country
existed since the beginning of the ICFTU, and there was sympathy for Reuther's position. Nevertheless, the ICFTU hesitated
in acting upon Reuther's request, partly because admitting a
recently split organization was regarded by some as a different
problem from that of admitting organizations which existed independently for a long time before affiliation with the ICFTU.
Others were concerned about the loss of income for the international organization resulting from the possible withdrawal of
the AFL-CIO if the UAW were accepted into membership. In the
end the ICFTU alienated both sides. Meany, criticizing the IC-
FTU for not having rejected the UAW application immediately,
announced that his organization was withdrawing from the international organization. The UAW, disappointed at not being admitted with open arms, withdrew its application and indicated
that it would concentrate its international activities within
the International Metalworkers' Federation rather than the
ICFTU.

Once again relations between the American unions and the international organization of democratic labor reached an impasse, although negotiations continued. In 1970 the AFL-CIO demanded successfully that the U.S. government withhold its membership dues from the ILO because the latter had appointed a Russian as assistant director general, of whom there are five. This step further alienated the U.S. from the European unions, which were attempting to find some form of accommodation with their Eastern neighbors.

On a regional level the ICFTU appears to have more vitality than on a world scale. The European regional organization is carrying on interesting activities, with the ICFTU affiliates in the Common Market countries taking the initiative in setting up (in the spring of 1969) a European Confederation of Free Trade Unions. The African affiliates of the ICFTU are asking for the reactivation of their regional organization. ORIT, the Latin American organization, is carrying on despite the handicap that its identification with the U.S., the "colossus to the North," presents in the Western Hemisphere. Its labor education center in Cuernavaca, Mexico, maintains a steady stream of activities.

Some international trade secretariats have so far succeeded in keeping out of most of the quarrels in the ICFTU. The largest of them, the International Metalworkers' Federation, is not far behind the ICFTU in the scope of its work. Yet the divisions in the wider movement threaten to have an impact on all the international labor organizations of the Western world.

Little needs to be said in this context about the Socialist International. Although most of the leaders of the European unions affiliated with the ICFTU—as well as many outside Europe—continue to be members of the social democratic or labor parties of their countries, the center of gravity of the international labor movement is no longer in the Socialist International. A modest headquarters in London carries on an exchange of communication and views among the affiliated parties, but neither the material means at the disposal of the organization nor its moral authority enable it to engage in large-scale activities.

The WFTU, deprived of most of its non-Communist membership, moved its headquarters from Paris to more hospitable areas in Eastern Europe. Its influence has greatly diminished, especially as a result of the Soviet interventions in Hungary (1956) and Czechoslovakia (1968). The smallest of the three international trade union organizations, the International Federation of Christian Trade Unions (IFCTU), never presented real challenge to either of its two large competitors. With highly limited financial resources, it set up a few small-scale suborganizations. The most active of them is the Latin American Federation of Christian Trade Unions (CLASC: Confederacion La-

tinoamericana de Sindicalistas Cristianos), whose headquarters
is in Venezuela.   In Europe the Christian International has only a small membership limited to a few countries.   In 1968 the
Sixteenth Congress of the IFCTU changed the name of the organization to World Confederation of Labour (WCL) and accepted a
declaration of principles which, while retaining a reference to
the Christian heritage of the organization, opened the doors to
new members without regard to religious belief, race, or sex.
Relations with the free trade unions have improved to the point
where cooperation has become possible.

The break between the European and the U.S. unions has
resulted in stagnation or even decline of the international
movements of organized labor.   This fact contrasts sharply
with the rapid internationalization of business organizations,
as expressed, for instance, in the rise of the multinational
corporation.   For the time being, the international labor organizations are with few exceptions ill equipped to meet the
new problems created by the internationalization of business.

12

Unions in Developing Countries

It is obviously difficult to suggest generally valid propositions about labor movements in areas as diversified as those
lumped together under such labels as *developing countries*, the
Third World, or *underdeveloped areas*. They are divided not only by climate, history, and economic potential but also by cultural and religious differences, political and social systems,
and many other factors. Indeed, nearly the only common trait
is a low per capita income. And even from this point of view
the definition is rather arbitrary, because the upper limit can
be set at different levels. Nearly all propositions that may
be hazarded about labor movements in this large group of countries are subject to qualifications and exceptions, yet we will
attempt to suggest at least a few generalizations that are frequently valid and that might offer some insight into the problems many of these movements face.

First, it is unlikely that the evolution of these labor
movements will simply repeat that of the Western movements with
some time lapse. True, several of the older movements have
made and continue to make valiant attempts to influence their
younger colleagues and especially to have them follow the path
the older movement found successful. Indeed, in the former colonial territories the earliest labor movements were frequently
organized by unions in the motherland and more or less con-
sciously patterned in the shape of the latter. This stage,
however, usually came to an end when the anticolonial movements, of which labor organizations frequently formed one of
the main pillars, arose. After independence was achieved the
forms of labor action that emerged were quite different in most
respects from those of the industrialized West.

Thus in the former French colonies in Africa unions were
formed at first as branches of the confederations in France,
and in the British colonies representatives of the TUC endeavored to set up organizations after the British model. Some of
these still survive, but most were dramatically transformed

during the anticolonial struggle. The essence of this transformation was that the labor organizations became part or at
least close associates of the nationalist liberation movement,
and from then on their evolution proceeded along lines quite
different from those of their Western colleagues.

The main reasons for these basic differences in ideology,
system of organization, and objectives and methods used to attain them are the economic and social circumstances in which
the new movements arise and operate. For instance, there is
little doubt that the industrial take-off in Western Europe and
the U.S. occurred under incomparably more favorable conditions
than now exist in the countries of—say—Africa and Southeast-
ern Asia. Output per man-year in the latter parts of the world
is now almost certainly less than half of that of Western Europe a century and a half ago. The high growth rates of the
West during the last two centuries are unique in the recorded
history of mankind, and the capital equipment per worker was a
multiple of what is now available for many, if not most, of
the countries of the Third World today.[1] Overseas migration
greatly relieved labor market pressures in Europe. On the
whole, therefore, the transition into modern society was far
easier then compared with the difficulties now facing a large
part of the newly industrializing nations. In particular, the
relation between demand and supply of labor is likely to have
been (or to have become sooner) more favorable to labor in the
older nations, except of course for periods of depression.

In any case, the tradition of heavy emphasis on political
action that was created during the struggle for national independence persisted after political independence was achieved,
because traditions tend to outlive the conditions that created
them and because in most cases the political and economic conditions of the new nations operated in the same direction. One
of these conditions was and continues to be the necessity of the
modernizing forces that form the backbone of the nationalist
movement to find support among organizations that transcend the
tribal, religious, and linguistic divisions within the country.
Unions are often one of these forces. Indeed, in the many cases in which modernization was the result of a conflict between
different social groups, the unions, although weak by most
standards, because of their concentration in the main centers
of the country formed one of the main pillars of the modernization movement and of the political power that emerged from it.

---

[1]The main sources for these statements can be found in Simon
Kuznets, *Modern Economic Growth: Rate, Structure and Spread*
(New Haven, Conn.: Yale University Press, 1966), and his *Eco-
nomic Growth of Nations: Total Output and Production Structure*
(Cambridge: Harvard University Press, 1971).

Trade union leaders were frequently more interested in political issues than in bread-and-butter unionism. In contrast
to the early history of large parts of Western labor, union
leadership in the new countries did not arise from the ranks of
artisans and skilled craftsmen who felt threatened by the rise
of more modern industrial establishments.[2] Because the new
factories gathered a disparate labor force with little education, the workers were compelled to look for leadership among
the intelligentsia.[3] These leaders viewed the labor problems
not as those of small occupational or industrial groups but
rather as those of a social and political system in which colonialism and capitalism were closely identified. This identity was cemented by the fact that modern industry was indeed
most often represented by foreign-owned and foreign-managed
business enterprises headquartered in capitalistic countries.

Thus an alliance between unions and the government has become the rule rather than the exception in the Third World.
The unions accept political leadership on most issues, often
in exchange for the right to dues check-off, without which few
of them could survive. On the other hand, the ability of organized workers, concentrated in the urban centers, to exert
pressure on the government is far greater in most cases than
their ability to engage in prolonged industrial conflicts.

This results in many countries from the situation of the
labor market, which makes purely economic action a highly ineffective weapon for most workers. Unemployment and underemployment weaken labor's capacity to engage in effective bargaining.[4] Strikes of common labor are unlikely to succeed
when thousands of potential workers stand at the factory gate

----

[2]See, for instance, Robert A. Scalapino's chapter on Japan in
Labor and Economic Development, ed. Walter Galenson (New York:
John Wiley & Sons, 1959).

[3]This has been the subject of much criticism by Western observers and also by social historians of the newly industrializing
nations. India is a classic example. However, the role of intellectuals in the early stages of unionism in countries such
as Austria-Hungary or Czarist Russia is a fairly close parallel.

[4]The concept *underemployment* has been defined in various ways.
For our purposes a fairly simple definition may be sufficient:
workers desiring to work more hours than they are being offered
at the prevailing or slightly lower wage rate. A careful discussion of the unemployment and underemployment problem in one
part of the developing world can be found in Irv Beller, "Latin
America's Unemployment Problem," *Monthly Labor Review*, November
1970, pp. 3-10.

willing to work at the current or a lower wage rate. Indeed,
the most obvious question that arises under such circumstances
is why competition for scarce jobs does not drive wage rates
close to zero.[5] Workers whose skills are rare may succeed in
obtaining wage advantages by collective bargaining, but the
large mass of unskilled workers cannot do so. Yet the formation of separate unions of skilled workers, although not total-
ly absent, is rendered difficult by the general climate of
class and often national solidarity, especially in the face of
a foreign-owned company. The most obvious way to obtain advantages is legislation or government pressure on foreign-owned
companies.[6] Moreover, increases in money wages are often regarded as unsatisfactory ways of improving living standards.
There is heavy emphasis on housing, medical care, sanitation,
and schooling as fringe benefits of employment—more often imposed by the government than by pressure of the workers themselves. Most important is minimum wage legislation, and changes in the minimum wage are often accompanied or followed rather
closely by corresponding adjustments of the entire wage structure. The primary direction of labor movements under those
conditions is thus frequently in the hands of the political
leaders.

In terms of organization this relationship is expressed
in a variety of ways. In Mexico the main union confederation
(CTM: Confederacion de Trabajadores Mexicanos) is an organic
part of the ruling party of Revolutionary Institutions. There
are other confederations, but most of them play an insignificant role compared with that of the CTM. The Chilean Trade Union Confederation (CUT: Central Unica de Trabajadores) is predominantly under Communist control. Where military dictatorships have been established—as in several Latin American countries in the sixties—they have usually assumed control of the
unions, with the outstanding exception of Argentina. There the
followers of the former dictator Juan Perón—or rather, those
who claim to be his disciples—continue to exert considerable
influence in the ranks of labor. India, at the other extreme,
has a variety of trade union centers, each connected with a political party. The Indian National Trade Union Congress (IN-
TUC) is closely identified with the government Congress party.

---

[5]This has been the subject of prolonged debates among economists. The most plausible answer—apart from institutional
factors still to be discussed—is the disutility of work, especially in conjunction with low nutrition levels.

[6]With the result that quite often differential wages and working conditions are imposed upon native and foreign establishments, mostly by different standards of enforcement.

The Socialist party in turn controls a union confederation, and so do other political organizations from time to time. In most of the new African countries one-party systems have been established in which outright party control of the unions is openly proclaimed.[7]

Economic circumstances greatly enhance the role of the government and consequently of politics in industrial relations. In many of the new countries the government is by far the largest single employer. Wage rates and conditions set by the government thus automatically assume primary importance. Moreover, they often set the pattern for the private economy, so that the negotiations with the government have fundamental importance for the entire economy.[8]

"Planning" has become the fashion in the developing countries, although the data for formulating even moderately precise plans and the administrative machinery necessary to implement them are highly defective. Yet planning at least focuses attention on the need of getting data, of establishing an adequate administration, and of providing means for rational policy-making. Inevitably the government plays a crucial role in all of these tasks. The nature of union-government relations thus assumes crucial importance, at least for the unions.

---

[7]For some parts of Africa some scholars have questioned that the close relationship between unions and political parties described in the text exists. Thus Elliot Berg and Jeffery Butler in *Political Parties and National Integration in Tropical Africa*, ed. James Coleman and Carl Rosberg (Berkeley and Los Angeles: University of California Press, 1964). The opposite view is held by Bruce Millen, "The Political Role of Labor in Developing Countries," (Washington, D.C.: Brookings Institution, 1963), and many other authors. Galenson put the issue in succinct terms: . . . "The outlook for nonpolitical unionism in the newly developing countries is not bright. We may expect, rather, a highly political form of unionism, with a radical ideology. Indeed, so strong is the presumption that this will be the prevailing pattern that, where it is absent, we may draw the conclusion that unionism is, in fact, subordinated to the employer or to the state, i.e., we are dealing either with company unionism or a labor front" (*Labor and Economic Development*, p. 8). We might add a reference to the powerful role that corruption plays in making union leaders serve the ends of the governing party in many countries.

[8]In some countries industry is pressured by the government to follow its pattern. In others arbitrary adoption of the government rates may be a substitute for scarce management talent.

WAGES POLICY

Government wages policy is one of the pillars on which development policy in general is based. There are of course collective agreements, sometimes patterned after those of developed countries.[9] However, very few of these agreements are the
result of genuine bargaining by two relatively evenly matched
partners. The unions are usually far too weak for effective
bargaining. Their position is undermined by a massive labor
surplus, by lack of funds, and by their members' extreme poverty. Even written agreements are often the result of government pressures.[10] The government may give selected unions
closed-shop privileges or may enable them in some other way to
restrict access to jobs. Other, more subtle forms of government intervention in favor of or against a union can be dis-
covered, often without too much difficulty, by an experienced
observer. Most cases of genuine bargaining without government
pressure concern skilled workers, whose supply in relation to
demand is limited by educational and other restrictions. For
the unskilled workers, the population explosion characteristic
of developing countries provides increasing competition and
thus further removes the moment when they could engage effectively in genuine collective bargaining.

Government wages policy is guided by a number of frequently contradictory considerations. Economic necessity requires
keeping the lid on wages to free resources for capital formation. The political interest of the government in many cases
favors a policy of befriending at least substantial parts of
the organized workers, who are in a strategic position in the
urban centers, where the major political decisions are being
made. Where the governments are weak and in fear of left-wing
attacks, politics often win out over economics. When the proportion of unionized workers is small relative to the total
population, the economic costs of such a policy may appear low
in view of the risk of political upheavals; indeed, because the
latter may prove costly in economic terms, it may be possible

---

[9]The first collective agreement in the Mexican cotton textile
industry was simply a translation of the "Wolverhampton price
list," as the principal British agreement of the time was
called. The only significant difference was a considerable
reduction of the work load per employee because new industrial
workers would not be expected to match the performance of their
experienced British colleagues.

[10]Compulsory arbitration, restrictions on strikes, and lockouts
are frequent. Whether these work for or against the workers
depends on political and economic circumstances.

to justify such a policy on economic grounds as well. This may
help explain why real wage increases for organized workers
quite often exceed productivity increases by a significant mar-
gin.

One of the consequences of such a policy is inevitably a
restraint on industrial employment and an emphasis on more
capital-intensive investment than relative factor availability
would suggest. This effect is increased by low "real" interest
rates—that is, interest rates that take into account the high
rates of inflation—which may even cause negative real interest rates. The wage differentials between the employed unionized workers and the rest are often exceedingly high, far higher than in advanced industrial nations. Although some part of
the differential may reflect the rarity of certain skills, most
of the difference is related to government policy—that is, the
establishment of some form of closed shop or other institutions
that isolate some working-class groups from competitive influences. The result is a widening of wage differentials in spite
of substantial unemployment in the urban centers. However,
some of these differentials are of a somewhat peculiar nature.
Legal minimum wages often raise the floor high above what one
would expect if the labor market were free to operate; family
allowances and seniority increments often outweigh skill differentials and establish a wage structure quite different from
what economic considerations would lead one to expect.

The objective of stability of employment has a high pri-
ority for both management and labor. For management, stable
employment means a reliable supply of experienced labor and
economies in training costs. For workers, job protection in a
labor market with excess supplies of labor is of vital importance. One result—the seniority supplement—has been mentioned.
Another result is a system of severance pay which provides for
increases in proportion to the length of service. After fifteen or twenty years on a job a worker's severance pay may
reach a level that makes dismissal practically impossible.[11]
Wages in kind—often indispensable when plants are established
away from urban centers—are a substantial part of compensation
and a powerful means of maintaining a stable labor force.

In many developing countries organized labor thus tends to
become a kind of workers' aristocracy in spite of low income
levels by Western standards. However, apart from a relatively
small number of skilled workers, only a tiny portion of organized labor owes its special status to genuine bargaining. The
power of the government is the determining force behind the

---

[11]Outstanding examples can be found in most Latin American
countries.

paper cover of whatever collective agreements exist.[12] There are, of course, underdeveloped countries in which neither unemployment nor underemployment is a significant problem; in some the rate of population increase may nevertheless create difficulties, even though the absolute level or, better, the labor-land ratio may be favorable. In these areas Western-style unionism and collective bargaining prove far easier to operate, once an acceptable level of literacy has been attained among at least a significant part of the workers.

Sharp debates have occurred among observers and within the developing countries themselves whether a policy of substantially rising real wages is compatible with the desire of the same countries to advance their development as rapidly as possible. Resources devoted to wage payments as a rule contribute little or nothing to capital formation because they are usually consumed. Capital formation—particularly in the heavy doses required for the "big push"—is thus hampered. The most outspoken view of what functions unions may thus perform and, even more, should not perform if economic development at rapid rates is to be achieved has been presented by Asoka Mehta, one of the most influential Indian economists.[13] Contrary to the consumptionist role that unions rightfully play in advanced industrial nations, their task in developing countries is to restrain wage demands. For "any attempt to increase consumption of the population is likely to generate inflationary pressure, . . . [which] may lead to reduction in exports due to rising costs of commodities and the frittering away of resources on foreign imported goods." And elsewhere in the same article:

> The restriction on consumption is most vital since any undue increase in the demand for consumers' goods or semi-necessities manufactured indigenously or imported from abroad may put an immediate pressure on the price-level as a result of demand outpacing the supply. Owing to the general physical bottlenecks that prevent the supply equating the demand, the pressure pushes the prices high enough to disturb the price-cost basis of a development plan. With a view toward holding the levels of income, price, and cost, the restriction on consumption is most essential.

---

[12]To preach collective bargaining and nonpolitical unionism to workers in the Third World is in most cases a futile exercise under the circumstances.

[13]Asoka Mehta, "The Mediating Role of the Trade Union in Underdeveloped Countries," *Economic Development and Cultural Change* 6, no. 1 (October 1957): 18-19.

Such a restriction, moreover, is essential from another point of view, viz., in raising the size of
savings necessary for capital formation.

In summary, "the role the trade unions can most usefully
play may be as follows: (1) observing self-imposed wage restraint on all levels; (2) educating their members to give up
extra-spendthrift habits of the labor class; (3) encouraging
small-savings among the classes [sic]; (4) increasing the labor
productivity through propaganda; (5) settling the differences
through the legally instituted machinery based on the principles of conciliation and/or arbitration; (6) helping the dis-
placed labor thrown out of employment as a result of rationali-
zation by inducing them to take training in new skills in the
institutions set up by the Government or State management; (7)
initiating cooperative action in the enforcement of minimum
wages; (8) inducing the labor class to effectively participate
in social security and provident fund schemes; and (9) sharing
in the profits on an acceptable basis which, while apportioning
a significant percentage of profit to labor, will leave sufficient incentive to the management to plow the profits back into
the industries they own."

This view has not remained unchallenged, in both the literature and the practice of trade unions and governments.[14]
Some doubts have been raised as to the size of the impact of
unions on resource allocation—doubts that have been sharpened
by studies indicating how uneven the income distribution appears to be in many developing countries and how vast the luxury expenditures are at the upper end of the income ladder.[15]

---

[14]Some examples of the vast literature on the subject are Galenson's introduction to a volume edited by him, *Labor in Developing Economies* (Berkeley and Los Angeles: University of California Press, 1962); my short comments, "Unions and Economic
Development," *Economic Development and Cultural Change* 8, no. 2
(January 1960); Paul Fisher, "The Economic Role of Unions in
Less Developed Areas," *Monthly Labor Review* 84, no. 9 (September 1961); and Solomon B. Levine's review of the discussion,
"Conceptions of Trade Unionism in Economic and Political Devel-
opment," *Economic Development and Cultural Change* 12, no. 2
(January 1964).

[15]The United Nations Economic Commission for Latin America
(ECLA) has carried on extensive investigations of the degree of
unevenness of income distribution in Latin America and has come
to the conclusion that in several countries of the region the
degree of unevenness vastly exceeds that of the U.S. This does
not yet prove that such unevenness is not favorable to capital

Moreover, by facilitating the transition of preindustrial workers into modern enterprises and urban life, the unions may add
as much or more to GNP than they subtract by their consumptionist activities. A good deal of union work in the early stages
of modernization is devoted to combating traditional discrimination against manual labor, and this may pay off in enlarged
production. Some degree of union pressure on entrepreneurs
may, in the absence of competitive product markets, stimulate
their inventiveness, although the same circumstances may have
the opposite effect: employers and union may combine in monopolistic exploitation of consumers.

Studies have attempted to demonstrate and measure the impact of improvements in the quality of the labor force on economic growth in developing countries. Although it is impossible to relate these changes in any convincing way to union
impact on wage levels or wage differentials, this discussion
may nevertheless make some contribution to the debate on union
influence on economic development.[16]

Since the debate on the "residual factor" in economic
growth started a decade or so ago, the contribution of education has loomed increasingly large. Given the high increase
of population in many developing countries, measurement must
extend to both the maintenance of a given proportionate level
of schooling—that is, its extension to an increasing absolute
number of people—and the advance of that level. By making a
number of rather stringent and alternative assumptions, one
author has estimated that the average rates of return to investment in human resources are high in the four countries he
examined—Mexico, Chile, Colombia, and Venezuela—high even
relative to the high rate of return to physical capital pre-

---

[15](Cont'd) formation, however, even though for social reasons
one might accept Joan Robinson's questioning of a system which
requires providing large enough incomes for a small group so
that it is willing to devote some part of them to capital
formation. Displays of extreme luxury consumption and consequent waste of resources can be found in many underdeveloped
countries. Whether or not this waste is a significant economic
factor, it undoubtedly weakens the moral position of the advocates of union restraint.

[16]It should be noted, however, that the leading study in the
field makes the assumption that wages reflect marginal produc-
tivities. We may thus be moving in a circle—admittedly one in
which national income accounting would keep us company. See
Marcelo Selowsky, "On the Measurement of Education's Contribution to Growth," *Quarterly Journal of Economics* 83, no. 3 (August 1969): 449-63, especially p. 450.

vailing in Latin America. This seems to apply especially to
primary and university education in countries of rapid economic
development. Expressed differently, this and other investigations seem to indicate that education—that is, a more highly
skilled labor force—has contributed at least as much to economic growth as investment in capital goods.[17]

More important perhaps are the noneconomic advantages successful unions may provide. They are training schools for administrative leaders in the newly industrializing countries;
their achievements "serve as the very symbol of change sought
by the emerging economy."[18] No less important may be the fact
that union organization and achievements may contribute to the
political stability of countries in which the armed forces are
otherwise almost the only source of indigenous power. It is
true, of course, that Communist groups of the most varied ideological shades—Maoists, Trotskyites, Stalinites, and so on—
have obtained control of labor organizations in many countries
of the Third World and have contributed to instability.

Where trade union influence leads—to economic advancement
with political stability or to retarded economic growth with
increasing mass dissatisfaction and political upheavals—is difficult if not impossible to establish by theoretical analysis.
Labor impact, as we have seen, is rarely limited to the economic sphere. It affects many aspects of life and development,
although the total effect may be rather small because of poverty, the small size of the nonagricultural labor force, and
the lack of experience of the labor leaders. Not only are labor movements in the developing countries different from those
in advanced industrial nations or from those in such countries
as the Soviet Union, which have passed the take-off stage, they
are also highly diversified among themselves, and they change
in many aspects from time to time. More often than not these
changes are imposed upon them rather than being the result of
their own decisions. Thus we are confronted by "drives for national identity in the case of Indonesia and Israel, . . . the
political vicissitudes of Argentina, Brazil, and Chile, the
need for unification that faces a divided Pakistan, and the
conflicts engendered in the transition from one-party to two-

---

[17]Martin Carnoy, "Rates of Return to Schooling in Latin America," *Journal of Human Resources* 2, no. 3 (Summer 1967). While
this was being written Joseph R. Ramos's book *Labor and Development in Latin America* (New York: Columbia University Press,
1970), came to my attention. Ramos's emphasis on the improvement of the quality of the labor force in Latin America appears to confirm the conclusions presented above.

[18]Levine, "Conceptions of Trade Unionism," p. 217.

party control in the case of Turkey. Out of these themes, one senses the close integration of unionism and other institutions in Israel and Indonesia, the institutional volatility of unions in the Latin American countries, and the almost complete isolation of labor organization in the make-up of Turkey and Pakistan."[19]

We must add two points to this discussion. One is a warning. Most of the considerations refer to developing countries with large labor surpluses. Only there does the reasoning related to "economic development with unlimited supplies of labor," to quote the title of W. Arthur Lewis's celebrated article,[20] fully apply. There are developing countries with factor proportions that are far more favorable to labor than—say—the crowded areas of South and Southeast Asia or the countries of Central America, in which the rate of population increase and the ratio of urban to rural population is exceedingly high. Even the latter do not necessarily come under the heading "unlimited supplies" of labor, but the rate of increase of the dependency ratio creates staggering problems for economic growth when measured in terms of per capita income.

The second required supplementary remark refers to the ideological character of labor movements in the Third World. We have repeatedly pointed out that the conditions for successful and genuine collective bargaining of the "ideal" Anglo-American style are rarely present in the developing countries. (Nor does the reality of the United States and the United Kingdom correspond too closely to the ideal.) The ideology of business unionism has little relevance under the circumstances. Efforts to transfer it to areas where material advances for the workers are necessarily modest and the effectiveness of collective bargaining generally dubious are bound to fail. Whatever the merits of free private and competitive enterprise in advanced industrial nations, the system holds little appeal to farm workers or even to those working in modern industries in the Third World. The record of Socialist or Communist ideas has been spotty. Japan and India have demonstrated most interest in Marxian socialism of various shades, ranging from democratic socialism to Leninist and Maoist theories. The Maoist variety has shown a degree of appeal in several countries, which becomes more readily understandable in the light of the fact that in their effort at economic modernization the Chinese

---

[19]Ibid., p. 219.

[20]*The Manchester School of Economic and Social Studies* 22, no. 2 (May 1954); also "Unlimited Labour: Further Notes," *The Manchester School of Economic and Social Studies* 26, no. 1 (January 1958).

peasants are closer than is the Soviet Union to the situation
in which most of the Third World finds itself today.

More significant perhaps is the development of a Socialist
ideology which is deliberately and outspokenly non-Marxian.
One of its main expressions is African socialism. Its starting
point is that, because they have not developed class divisions
and class conflicts, African societies do not lend themselves
to either the Marxian analysis of pre-Socialist societies nor
consequently to Marx's laws of social dynamics, whose basis is
class conflict. An official White Paper on African socialism
issued by the government of Kenya states:

> The sharp class divisions that once existed in Europe
> have no place in African Socialism and no parallel
> in African society. No class problem arose in the
> traditional African society and none exists today
> among Africans. The class problem in Africa, there-
> fore, is largely one of prevention.[21]

From this fact it follows that the main task of Socialist
construction in Africa is work—the obligation for all persons
to work for the development of one's society. For trade unions
the same report stipulates:

> Government will assist trade unions to become in-
> volved in economic activities such as cooperatives,
> housing schemes, training schemes, workers' disci-
> pline and productivity, and in general, to accept
> their social responsibilities.[22]

Only the future can show whether African socialism is
more than an appealing cover for the harsh necessities the re-
alities of African life impose upon any government, whether
genuinely devoted to rapid economic modernization of the primi-
tive economic and social systems existing in vast parts of that
continent or simply interested in remaining in power.

---

[21]*African Socialism and Its Application in Kenya* (Nairobi: Republic of Kenya, 1965), p. 12, as quoted in Kassalow, *Trade Unions and International Relations*, p. 316.

[22]Ibid., p. 56. There is a fairly large literature on African
socialism. A good survey is William H. Friedland and Carl Rosberg, Jr., eds., *African Socialism* (Stanford, Calif.: Stanford
University Press, 1964). Albert Camus' book *The Rebel* (New
York: Alfred A. Knopf, 1954) offers important insights, as
does, in a very different way, Adam B. Ulam's book, *The Unfin-
ished Revolution: An Essay on the Sources of Influence of Marxism and Communism*, (New York: Random House, 1960).

13

Labor in Socialist Countries

Limits of space permit only a brief introductory discussion of the intriguing and intricate problems that arose in the attempt to find the "proper" place for unionism in societies that call themselves Socialist or Communist. For many of them, especially for the Soviet Union, the fundamental problem at the beginning of the new regime was the same that confronts all preindustrial societies and those in the early stages of industrialization: how to acquire the real and human capital required for modernization of a backward country. Two elements were more specifically Russian: the need, for political reasons, to carry out the transformation of the country at a speed that appeared impossible in the light of historic experience, and the indispensable requirement of giving this process its rationale in the theory of Marxian socialism.

The literature here and abroad has paid considerable attention to Lenin's views about the role of the trade unions in the broader context of the Russian labor movement. In line with the predominant current within the (first and second) Socialist Internationals, Lenin held that "trade unions were not only legitimate but necessary as long as capitalism existed, . . . but they ought to strive for the general emancipation of the oppressed millions of the working people. . . ."[1] It was the task of the Socialists "to make the economic struggle of the workers assist the socialist movement and contribute to the success of the revolutionary socialist party."[2] Thus unions were to concentrate on the defense of the immediate interests of the workers or of working-class groups, and the Socialists

---

[1] Lenin, *Sochinenya* (Works), 4th ed., vol. 4, pp. 158-59; quoted by Isaac Deutscher, "Russia," in *Comparative Labor Movements*, ed. Walter Galenson (New York: Prentice-Hall, 1952), pp. 481-82.

[2] Ibid., p. 482.

were to lead them toward the overthrow of the capitalist system
as the ultimate condition of a real and permanent solution to
the workers' problems. Unions were to be mass organizations,
whereas the party was to be a small, well-disciplined organization of highly trained revolutionaries. This relationship corresponded roughly to the role Socialist students and intellectuals were playing in the textile strikes in the middle nineties. Another form of working-class organization which enabled
the Socialists to influence large numbers of workers arose
spontaneously during the revolution of 1905—the "soviets,"
workers' councils elected by all workers, whether unionized or
not. The weakness of workers' organizations prompted the creation of this new organizational structure.

Lenin's views were not shared by all Russian Social Democrats. Another Marxian group, the Mensheviks, opposed Lenin's
Bolsheviks because the Mensheviks, following the German model,
desired to develop Socialist mass organizations in Russia rather than an elite that would use the workers as its instrument
to attain its objectives. However, both groups agreed that
Russia was a backward country just entering the capitalistic
stage and thus far from ready for a Socialist revolution. Even
in 1917, when he was leaving his Swiss exile, in a farewell
letter to the workers of Switzerland Lenin expressed his conviction that Russia was a backward country which only an accident of history had placed in the forefront of the revolutionary movement; once the revolution was victorious in highly industrialized Germany, Russia would once again take its proper
place in the cavalcade of the revolutionary movement—namely
that of a backward country.[3] The first stage of the postrevolutionary regime can be understood only in the light of the expectation that a revolutionary Germany would soon assist Russia
in constructing a modern Socialist society. The "utopian" experiments in workers' control, collective management, and so on
arose out of this atmosphere of hope and illusion—an atmosphere that assisted the Bolsheviks, masters of the art of organization, to win control of the unions.

However, this merely set the stage for new and sharp debates, this time among the Bolsheviks themselves. What was to

---

[3]"We know perfectly well that the proletariat of Russia is less
organized, less prepared and less class-conscious than the proletariat of other countries. It is not its special qualities,
but rather the special conjuncture of historical circumstances
that *for a certain, perhaps very short*, time has made the proletariat of Russia the vanguard of the revolutionary proletariat of the whole world." Lenin, *Farewell Letter to the Swiss
Workers. Collected Works*, vol. 23, August 1916-March 1917 (London: Lawrence and Wishart, n.d.g.), p. 371. Italics by Lenin.

be the role of the trade unions in a country ruled by "your chosen Government, your Workers and Peasants Government"?[4]   In due course this question became inextricably intertwined with the struggle for power among Lenin's successors, which ended with the victory of Stalin over his rivals, and with the requirements of the rapid industrialization of the country.   Long before this, while the Bolshevik regime was still in its infancy, the role of the unions in a Socialist-dominated state was the object of debates at trade union and party congresses and especially in the party caucuses of the trade unions.   Syndcalist views of workers' control contended with forces eager to see the unions absorbed into the state machinery.[5]   The introduction of the New Economic Policy (NEP), which involved a certain amount of liberalization, led to a greater degree of management authority in the plant and some forms of collective bargaining.   Strikes did occur, but their number declined and became insignificant by 1928.   Although the Bolsheviks never dared to go so far as to declare strikes illegal—to this day they are officially legal—the foremost Bolshevik trade union leader, Nikolai Tomsky, stated that "we must root out all those who . . . still persist in organizing strikes against that government.   The unions which foment strikes . . . must suffer for it."[6]   Collective bargaining was permitted, but the ultimate weapon was denied the unions.   Indeed, the unions themselves were to enforce the strike prohibition.

Once the isolation of the Soviet Union and the failure of all Communist-inspired revolutions in Europe was acknowledged, the rapid transformation of the country from "a peasant country, one of the most backward of European countries"[7] to a modern industrial nation was regarded as a matter of life or death for the Bolsheviks.   The political loyalty of the peasants to the new regime was doubtful, even though it had given them the land, but the industrial workers were regarded as the natural support of the Bolshevik government.   To turn peasants and agricultural laborers into an industrial proletariat at breakneck

---

[4]G. Y. Zinoviev, as quoted in Jay B. Sorenson, *The Life and Death of Soviet Trade Unionism, 1917-1928* (New York: Atherton Press, 1969), pp. 29-30.

[5]Mary McAuley, *Labour Disputes in Soviet Russia, 1957-1965,* (Oxford: Clarendon Press, 1959), p. 10.

[6]Quoted in Sorenson, *Life and Death of Soviet Trade Unionism,* p. 37.   Lenin himself was less firm in identifying the unions with the state.

[7]Lenin, ibid.

speed became the foremost task of the regime. This in turn required rapid capital accumulation and thus the reduction of
consumption to the lowest level compatible with the security of
the regime. And because by their very nature unions have a
proconsumption bias, they had to be deprived of their power to
influence wages. Nor could they be permitted to interfere with
those forms of labor control—such as the allocation of work
places—which the execution of the successive five-year plans
(beginning in the late twenties) required. The removal of Tomsky from the trade union leadership in December 1928, in spite
of his loyalty to the party, and his replacement by Nikolai
Shvernik marked the complete submission of the unions to the
party. Even internal policy discussions were no longer permitted. The totalitarian system was firmly established, leaving
the unions only administrative functions in the social security
system and in the more or less compulsory recruitment of
skilled labor for the new and expanding factories. The unions
organized training programs for workers, for specific skills—
the factory schools—as well as for general education.[8]

"Socialist emulation" and incentive wage systems were further instruments of hothouse industrialization designed to stimulate higher productivity, sharply contrasting with the egali-
tarian trend of the early postrevolutionary era. Stakhanovism,
named after a coal miner who reportedly produced fourteen times
the normal output in a shift, became the model of the new workingman in a "Socialist" country. Trade union membership grew
by leaps and bounds, not only because the number of industrial
workers grew but also because union members had tremendous material advantages—for example, double sickness benefits.

The rise of nazism, the totalitarian terror, and World War
II and its frightful economic consequences produced "the black-
est period in Soviet labor relations."[9] All legal restraints
on management were either abolished or disregarded. Only gradually and slowly, beginning in 1947, were collective agreements
reintroduced, but their impact was negligible. As Nikita
Krushchev stated: "On all sides there is failure to carry out
the agreements, and the trade unions keep quiet as though
everything was quite in order."[10] Even in individual disputes
of highly limited economic significance, management often disregarded the legally prescribed procedures, and the trade unions only rarely entered into the handling of grievances.

---

[8]Deutscher, "Russia," pp. 542 ff.

[9]McAuley (*Labor Disputes in Soviet Russia*, p. 40) uses this
phrase but limits it to the Forties.

[10]Ibid., p. 43.

The Khrushchev period and the years following his downfall produced considerable fluctuations in the degree of centralization of economic management. Moreover, the progress of economic recovery, partly the result of growing autonomy at lower levels of decision-making, reduced the need for harsh restraints on consumption and thus on trade union activity. Yet a basic problem remained: plan fulfillment was the supreme task of management and the plan objectives of the enterprise were determined by the appropriate industrial branch of the regional economic administration (*sovnarkhoz*). This led to intricate games between the plant and *sovnarkhoz* in setting plant objectives. Still, wartime restrictions on leaving, transfer, and absenteeism were lifted—ten to fifteen years after the end of hostilities. Moreover, legislation enacted in 1957 and 1958 gave the union committee in the plant greater rights in grievance handling, required union agreement for various plant decisions, and led to the establishment of "permanent production conferences" of management, union, party and workers' representatives in the plants or plant departments.[11] While union structure—all unions cover the entire personnel of an industry —also tended to be less centralized to correspond to the increased emphasis on the regional autonomy of the economic administration, the interrelationship of union, management, and party was and remains such that the particular rights of any group can rarely be clearly defined. Indeed, personnel appear to be interchangeable from one group to another, so that the same person may appear with a different label at different times or even in different capacities on different committees at the same time. In other words, the same person may represent management and the union at different committee levels at any given time. This could be—favorably or naively—interpreted as a sign of high social mobility, were it not that at the top, where the fundamental decisions are made, the concentration on party personnel remains heavy.

SOCIALIST SYNDICALISM

After the break between the USSR and Yugoslavia in 1948, the economic system of the latter country underwent a radical reorientation. Until 1950-52 it was patterned after the Soviet model of centralized administrative management. With many fluctuations and a surprising willingness to experiment, the new trend has been in the direction of a decentralized Socialist market economy, with "free," although not private, enterprise as its slogan. Fiscal and monetary policies are deter-

---

[11]Ibid., p. 66.

mined by higher authority, and volume and direction of investment are influenced by these decisions, but even those matters
are increasingly referred to decentralized authorities.

The basic principles of the new system—preserved through
all its variations and experiments—are summarized in the term
workers' management. Enterprises are not nationalized in the
same way as in the Soviet Union or as electricity and gas are
nationalized in Great Britain and France. They are "social
property" managed by the elected representatives of the employees within the framework set by the fiscal and monetary decisions of the authorities. The latter operate on three levels
—the federal, the individual republic, and the local munici-
pality. The employees perform roughly the functions of stockholders in a corporation in the capitalistic system, or, better, those of the members of a producers' cooperative; they
elect a managerial board whose functions are somewhat comparable to those of a corporation board. It participates in the
election of the managing director and sets the general policies the director is to implement. However, although they
perform managerial functions, the members of the workers' council and of the management board are at the same time employees
of the enterprise. This combination of functions is the most
significant characteristic of the Yugoslav Socialist system and
is that which distinguishes it from the organization of Soviet
enterprises. The workers' incomes are at the same time wages
and shares in the surplus of the enterprise, insofar as the
surplus is not being used for investment.

Among the many problems with which the system had to cope
are some that are common to all or most countries undergoing
rapid industrialization and others that are specifically Yugoslav. The conflict with the Soviet Union and the desire to develop a different form of socialism; the reluctance to apply
Soviet-style bureaucratic methods such as physical and centralized planning of production and rationing of consumption; the
internal strains created by the friction among the various
provinces or "nationalities" of Yugoslavia, with their highly
diverse historical background accentuated by considerable dis-
crepancies in economic and cultural development, and many other
problems compelled the regime to seek solutions of its own that
are greatly at variance from other models of Socialist economies.

One of the most difficult of these problems was that of
incentives. The system of workers' management makes the director dependent on the good will and the cooperation of the workers rather than on the harsh methods of industrial management
common to the early stages of the formation of an industrial
work force. The problem was made even more difficult in the
early stages by the paucity of managerial talent and the modest
wages of managers relative to the earnings of skilled or even

unskilled workers. Management had to rely on persuasion, the
assistance of the workers' council, and the open or secret
pressure of the Communist party and its membership in the
plant. In the long run, however, the scarcity of managerial
talent and the increasing autonomy given the plants led to considerable and in some cases shocking improvements in the status
and living standards of managers relative to that of the workers.

In much the same way, material incentives became increasingly important as far as the work force was concerned. Piecework was used as far as possible from the beginning, and one of
the implications of workers' management was to establish a direct relationship between the productivity of a given plant and
the income of its work force. There were some distorting factors in this relationship, however. Monopolistic elements
played an important role in determining the financial results
of many enterprises, often a larger part than physical productivity. Yet gradually the individual enterprise acquired the
right to decide about the disposition of its profits, if it had
any. Fringe benefits, independent of the effort of the individual worker, represent a large part of his total compensation, far larger than in most industrial nations in Europe.

Perhaps the most puzzling aspect of "workers' management"
is how to fit the unions into the system. The main union functions in capitalistic countries, such as collective bargaining,
derive from a separation, not only functionally but also per-
sonally between the work force and management.[12] This distinction is difficult to apply in the Yugoslav system. The national or provincial union is an outside agency; the management
board and the workers' council are far closer to the work force
of the plant. The union section in the plant as a rule plays a
secondary role in the life of the Yugoslav worker. It nomi-
nates lists of candidates for the election of the council, but
it shares this right with other employee groups. It plays a
modest role in the handling of individual grievances and in the
approval of the wage schedule after it has been worked out by
the council. National agreements concluded by the union and
the appropriate industry association set minima and maxima for
different job categories. The union's main assignment is probably in the area of education, especially the training of council members.

If plant unions become active, they are likely to end up
in opposition to the union leadership at higher levels. The
more the plant union is identified with the concerns of the
low-income groups among the workers, the more involved it will

---

[12]Some blurring of this distinction occurs also in German codetermination.

be in strikes—which inevitably bring it into conflict with
provincial and federal authorities of all kinds—party, union,
or government. Moreover, the union section may contribute to
the sharp internal divisions of the country: in the advanced
parts of the country, the workers complain about the taxes they
have to pay for the benefit of the backward areas; unions in
the less developed areas believe that the high prices the workers have to pay for industrial products, inefficiently produced
in small and often badly located plants, represent exploitation
of backward areas by the workers in Croatia and Slovenia, the
industrially advanced provinces.

The union is thus in the unenviable position of being
either at the service of the establishment or an instrument of
division and rebellion. This dilemma is accentuated by the employment effects of the plant autonomy. Because the enterprise
behaves like a producers' cooperative, it will tend to restrict
employment to that point at which the increment in output resulting from the employment of an additional worker equals average output per worker—that is, where the per capita output
curve begins to slope downward. At that point, all other circumstances being equal, income per employed worker is at a maximum. In practice this often meant substantial layoffs and unemployment, another issue over which plant-union and higher
union echelons are at odds.

To some extent this problem coincides with that of finding
a proper balance between the powers of the central authorities
—whether they are those of the state or those of the individual republics—and the autonomy of the enterprise. Centralism
finds its support in the fear that left to itself, the work
force of the individual enterprises will consume too large a
portion of the revenue and thus devote inadequate resources to
investment and expansion. The inflationary tendencies characteristic of Yugoslavia for so long are referred to as evidence
that overconsumption is a real danger. In contrast, the advocates of plant autonomy claim that central bureaucracies are
wasteful and irresponsible and that only by confronting the results of their own actions will the workers acquire the self-
discipline indispensable for the function of the system.

In this area too the regional differences in the country
play a large and dangerous role. The educational level necessary for an understanding of the system and its implications
has not yet been reached by the workers of several areas. On
the whole the system works best in the large modern enterprises
concentrated in the north and northwest of Yugoslavia. In other areas technocrats enjoying the blessings of the party have
often substituted their own authority for that of the workers'
council, and with the union removed from the daily life of the
worker, democratic self-government is not much more than a
catch phrase. Indeed, the question may legitimately be asked

whether a one-party regime, even with a minimal level of suppression of opposing views, is conducive to the full development of democratic self-government in any essential sphere of social life.

14

Conclusion

The evolution of the labor movements in most Western industrialized nations since the end of World War II has shown a number of dominant, but in many cases contradictory, trends.

What is commonly called the generation gap has not spared the labor movements. The cement of class consciousness, which in Western and Central Europe tied skilled and unskilled workers together in one upsurge of emancipation, has little power as far as the younger generation of workers is concerned. The most obvious forms of discrimination to which the workers were subject fifty years ago have disappeared or have been weakened to the point where they no longer arouse the resentment of the great majority of workers. The labor movement, once an instrument of liberation from unbearable oppression, has increasingly been turned into a device for the continual improvement of material standards, which in most industrial nations have become quite comfortable. The labor movement must "deliver" to justify its existence; its character as a protest movement is less dominant in the functions of the movement and its appeal.

This trend has been reenforced by the changes in the structure of the labor force that have manifested themselves in different degrees in all industrialized nations. A labor movement limited to manual workers is in danger of stagnation or even decline. When it expands to include white-collar workers and especially professionals, it changes its character in fundamental ways. Class consciousness holds little appeal to these rapidly growing groups of the labor force. Although they hope that their organizations—often halfway houses between union and professional group—will help maintain or improve the social status of their occupation, they attach increasing importance to the material achievements of their organizations.

A further factor in promoting increased orientation toward the practical achievements of unionism has been the role of models of industrial relations in the post-World War II era. The leading model in the Western world has been the system of the United States, with its emphasis on collective bargaining, short-term policies, and material results. As a consequence, one of the most conspicuous features of the industrial relations scene has been the spread of collective bargaining throughout the industrial nations since World War II. It has acquired almost mystical qualities for manual workers and public opinion, although acceptance is still far short of unanimous for white-collar employees. Bargaining has also spread in a different sense—the subject matter covered by the agreements. Government regulation of collective bargaining has also made progress, not about the contents of agreements but primarily to regulate the process leading to the bargain. Governments are also groping toward methods of making industrial conflicts less painful for the general public, because the impact of strikes has become more severe as industrial societies have become urbanized and the division of labor has progressed.

Two directions of the expansion of unionism and collective bargaining deserve special mention. The first concerns public employees. In some countries, for example, France, they have long been unionized, although their collective bargaining systems vary from industry to industry. In other countries, assisted at various times by friendly governments, unionism has only recently spread to public employees, who in the past had been excluded from it. Even when such enlargement of the industrial territory of collective bargaining was hedged by restrictions on the use of some traditional union weapons such as the strike, events have often demonstrated that unionism tends to overcome limitations of its means of action imposed by law or tradition.

Almost everywhere in the West unionism has spread to white-collar workers, an ill-defined group of employees ranging from artists and engineers to office workers of modest skills. In line with their diversity, tradition, and sometimes simply historical accident, they respond in very different ways to the appeals of unionism. Equally diversified is the contribution they make to the labor movement as a whole and their impact on it, which hardly ever fits into the conventional ideological categories of right-wing and left-wing. One contribution of increasing importance in labor is the wealth of skill and technical competence white-collar workers can put at the disposal of the movement. More important still: white-collar groups are the most rapidly growing category among the gainfully employed. A labor movement without significant white-collar associates may be doomed to stagnation—numerically as well as intellectually. Making white-collar labor a valued associate of the movement gives it opportunities for expansion and new vitality.

On the Continent, although by no means in all countries, collective bargaining has expanded to a substantial extent by the conclusion of agreements on levels high above the plant.

Contracts between union confederations and employers' associations have taken on increased significance in France and Italy, while in West Germany a good deal of union energy has been devoted to the expansion of the codetermination system. Although it is closer to the plant than the interconfederal agreements in France and Italy, the German union offensive still aims at strengthening union influence at managerial levels and by direct union participation in management decision-making, a course of action rejected by unions in Great Britain and the United States. For the latter bargaining rather than participation in management is the proper function of unions.

The first group of unions—most of whom are domiciled on the Continent—operate at the higher levels of public administration and business management. The designation "administrative union" may be appropriate. The fact that they were excluded from in-plant activities by the creation of separate in-plant institutions or the resistance of employers may help explain the direction they have taken. U.S. and many British unions, on the other hand, are firmly established in the plant and refuse to accept any share of managerial responsibility. Their activity consists predominantly in bargaining, a term which includes grievance handling.

Both types of unions, bargaining and administrative—differentiated more by emphasis than by a clear-cut distinction—have been led by circumstances to reconsider their strategies and systems of organization. The main factor causing this painful process of self-criticism was (and, I suspect, will remain for some time to come) full employment as a more or less permanent feature of the economic, social, and political landscape of the industrialized nations.

For all unions full employment has created two problems whose solution seems to lead in opposite directions. The spread between contract and effective wages—in the broadest meaning of the term—has caused the development of what the Donovan Commission pointed out is a dual industrial relations system. One operates at the level of the national agreement and usually represents not much more than a floor for wages, fringes, and conditions. The other system sets the effective rates and functions at the level of the enterprise or even the plant. This has occurred in Britain and in most Continental countries. However, the problem requires different solutions for the bargaining unions than for the administrative unions. For the countries of the bargaining unions, contrary to what public opinion demands, the main task seems to be to strengthen the authority of the unions vis-à-vis the shop stewards in order for the dual system to disappear. This involves not only a change in the basic structure of collective bargaining but also of the unions themselves. Plant-wide agreements must be concluded by, or at least under the supervision of, the national unions, so that the shop stewards are reduced to the role they were intended to have—namely, that of enforcing the union-sponsored agreement and applying it to the particular conditions of a plant or department. To fulfill their task the national unions need far more financial resources than they have—for example, in Britain—and a favorable climate of public opinion. Neither of these conditions appears to be met at this time.

Yet even if the effort of reducing the dual bargaining system to one system were to succeed, the bargaining unions would still be confronted by the problem of how their function could be fitted into a set of broader economic policies aiming at a higher measure of price stability and the avoidance of balance-of-payments crises. Probably we will have to be modest in our expectations of what unions—especially bargaining unions—can contribute. In the report of the German Council of Experts to Advise on the General Economic Evolution, submitted in November 1970, a paragraph devoted to this problem deserves quotation:

> A strategy aiming at bringing the evolution of the economy back to equilibrium, cannot rest on wages policy. The state can give good advice to the social partners [the standard German expression for management and unions together—A.S.] in their determination of wages, but not more than advice. And the incomes policy of the social partners cannot be business cycle policy. One can only induce the social partners to behave according to the requirements of the business cycle if fiscal and credit policy are successful in securing a balanced economic evolution. The responsibility for a return to the path of equilibrium . . . rests with economic policy, not with the social partners.[1]

Still, as citizens contributing to the formulation of government economic policy and exposed to its consequences, the union members and their organizations find it increasingly difficult to formulate their policies without regard for the impact of those policies on society at large and the impact of government policies on their own strategy. The power of the unions and the impact changes in public opinion may have on them compel even unions deeply committed to playing the role of a private interest group to consider the wider framework within which they operate. From such considerations small steps lead

---

[1] *Annual Report of the Council of Experts* (Bonn, Germany: November 30, 1970), para. 301, p. 86.

toward attempts to influence public economic policies in a direction favorable to the outcome of future bargaining.

This trend is greatly enhanced by the attempts to combat inflation by some form of wage restraint. What has politely been called incomes policy logically requires the determination of an entire set of economic policies into which incomes policies need to be fitted. This recognition has caused different reactions among unions, not only in different countries but even within the same country. Some have refused to share the responsibilities that in their view must be borne by political parties and the government rather than by a particular interest group. Others have raised preliminary conditions for the acceptance of social responsibilities, often in the full knowledge that their conditions would be rejected. Yet the evolution seems to make such positions increasingly difficult to maintain. The risk that public opinion will turn against the unions is great. Reluctantly but steadily bargaining unions are led to enlarge their horizons.

Administrative unions, whose main impact is aimed at top policy-making bodies and whose leverage has been traditionally strongest above the plant level and within top plant management, are desperately trying to strengthen their power position by taking root in the plant itself. They intend to continue and to expand their participation in policy-making bodies above the plant level, especially in government planning agencies, their bargaining with employers' associations on an industry-wide basis, and wherever possible, their role in plant management, as in German codetermination. Yet they increasingly feel the need to strengthen their base in the plant. In France an opportunity for this exists, because the Grenelle protocol and its sequel may have facilitated union operations in the plant. In Germany and other countries works' councils, which are at least legally and quite often in fact independent of the union, stand in the way of expansion of union organization and activity at the work place. There is no clear indication yet how these problems can be solved. There is little doubt, however, that their solution is a vital condition for unions whose main level of operations has so far been either in plant management or in areas above the plant.

If the evolution of Western unionism were to proceed in these directions, the distinction between bargaining and administrative unions—which even now is mainly one of emphasis rather than a clear contrast—could tend to diminish. However, because unions in most countries are old and tradition-bound organizations, their resistance to change is exceedingly strong —so strong, in fact, that the danger that they will be bypassed by events can never be disregarded.

Bibliography

As a guide to further study we list a small number of books which will assist the reader in locating further sources of information. Such a small selection is unavoidably arbitrary and should not be taken, even inferentially, as a judgment of the quality of books not listed.

Allen, V. L. *Power in Trade Unions*. London, New York: Longmans Green, 1954.

Clegg, Hugh A. *General Union: A Study of the National Union of General and Municipal Workers*. London, Oxford: Blackwell, 1954.

Cole, G.D.H. *A History of the Labour Party from 1914*. London: Routledge & Kegan-Paul, 1948.

_____. *A Short History of the British Working Class Movement, 1789-1947*. New York: George Allen and Unwin, 1948.

Cyriax, George, and Robert Oakeshott. *The Bargainers*. London: Faber and Faber, 1960.

Dunlop, John. *Industrial Relations Systems*. New York: Holt, 1958.

Flanders, Allan, and Hugh Clegg. *The System of Industrial Relations in Great Britain*. London, Oxford: Blackwell, 1954.

Galenson, Walter. *Trade Union Democracy in Western Europe*. Berkeley and Los Angeles: University of California Press, 1961.

_____, ed. *Comparative Labor Movements*. New York: Prentice-Hall, 1952.

Goldstein, Joseph. *The Government of British Trade Unions*. London: George Allen and Unwin, 1952.

Horowitz, Daniel. *The Italian Labor Movement*. Cambridge: Harvard University Press, 1963.

Johnson, T. L. *Collective Bargaining in Sweden*. Cambridge: Harvard University Press, 1962.

Kassalow, Everett. *Trade Unions and Industrial Relations: An International Comparison*. New York: Random House, 1969.

165

Kerr, Clark, Frederick H. Harbison, John T. Dunlop, and Charles A. Myers. *Industrialism and Industrial Man*. Cambridge: Harvard University Press, 1960.

Knoellinger, C. E. *Labor in Finland*. Cambridge: Harvard University Press, 1960.

La Palombara, Joseph. *The Italian Labor Movement*. Ithaca, N.Y.: Cornell University Press, 1947.

Levine, Solomon B. *Industrial Relations in Postwar Japan*. Urbana: University of Illinois Press, 1958.

Lorwin, Val R. *The French Labor Movement*. Cambridge: Harvard University Press, 1954.

Perlman, Selig. *A Theory of the Labor Movement*. New York: Augustus M. Kelley, 1949.

Ross, Arthur M. "Prosperity and Labor Relations in Europe: The Case of West Germany." *Quarterly Journal of Economics* 76, no. 3 (August 1962), pp. 63-85.

Schumpeter, Joseph. *Capitalism, Socialism, and Democracy*. New York: Harper & Row, 1947.

Sturmthal, Adolf. *Workers Councils*. Cambridge: Harvard University Press, 1964.

_____. "The Labor Movement Abroad." In *A Decade of Industrial Relations Research 1946-1956: An Appraisal of the Literature in the Field*, edited by Neil W. Chamberlain et al. New York: Harper & Row, 1958.

_____, ed. *Contemporary Collective Bargaining*. Ithaca, N.Y.: Cornell University Press, 1957.

_____. *Unity and Diversity in European Labor*. Glencoe, Ill.: The Free Press, 1953.

Taira, Koji. *Economic Development and the Labor Market in Japan*. New York: Columbia University Press, 1970.

Turner, H. A., and Zoeteweij, H. *Prices, Wages, and Incomes Policies*. Geneva: International Labor Organization, 1966.

Webb, Sidney, and Webb, Beatrice. *The History of Trade Unionism*. New York: Longmans, Green and Co., 1920.

_____. *Industrial Democracy*. London and New York: Longmans, Green and Co., 1920.

Windmuller, John P. *Labor Relations in the Netherlands*. Ithaca, N.Y.: Cornell University Press, 1969.

_____. *American Labor and the International Labor Movement, 1940-1953*. Ithaca, N.Y.: Cornell University Press, 1955.

Index

absolutism, 2, 6, 7, 8, 112
Accords de Grenelle, 84, 85
"administrative" unions, 43-47,
  50, 55, 71, 89, 96, 162, 164
AFL (U.S.), 131-32, 133
AFL-CIO, 134, 135, 136
Africa, 90, 134, 136, 139, 142,
  142n, 150
African-American Labor Center
  (AALC), 134, 136
African socialism, 150
agricultural protectionism, 10n
Amalgamated Society of Engineers
  (Britain), 19, 20
American Institute for Free Labor
  Development (AIFLD), 134
Anarchists. See syndicalism;
  Syndicalists
Anarcho-Syndicalists. See syndi-
  calism; Syndicalists
anticlericalism, 40
Argentina, 141, 148
artisan, 4, 5
Asia, 90, 134, 139, 149
Australia, 32n
Austria, 131
  civil service in, 112, 113
  foreign workers in, 74
  nationalization in, 101, 105
  Socialists in, 103, 105
  union membership in, 48
  union-party relations in, 21,
    24, 31
  voting rights in, 3
Austria-Hungary, 3, 88, 140n. See
  also Austria

Bad Godesberg Congress, 40
Bakunin, Mikhail, 25

balance-of-payments crisis, 116,
  120, 122
"bargaining" unions, 43-47, 55,
  162, 163, 164
Bauer, Otto, 103, 105, 106
Bebel, August, 14
Belgium, 21, 113, 134
Bernhard, Georg, 13
Bernstein, Eduard, 13-14
Besant, Annie, 13
Beveridge, William H., 115, 119
Bevin, Ernest, 59, 104
Biedenkopf Commission (West Ger-
  many), 72
Bismarck, Otto von, 7, 22
"black wages" (Netherlands), 123,
  127
Blanc, Louis, 5
blue-collar workers:
  decline of, 34
  in France, 97
  in labor organizations, 35
  in U.S., 35
  in West Germany, 72, 93
Blum, Léon, 28, 77, 78
Boeckler, Hans, 66
Bolshevik Revolution, 132. See
  also Russian Revolution
Bolsheviks, 15-16, 18, 152-53
Bömelburg, Theodor, 22
Bourses du Travail (France), 25
Brandt, Willy, 95
Braun, Heinrich, 13
Brazil, 148
Brenner, Otto, 47, 125
Britain, 5, 12n, 13, 138, 143n,
  149
  "bargaining" unions in, 43, 44,
    55

167

168 Index